A HISTORY OF THE COUNTY DUBLIN

THE PEOPLE, PARISHES AND ANTIQUITIES FROM THE EARLIEST TIMES TO THE CLOSE OF THE EIGHTEENTH CENTURY

PART FIRST

Being a History of that portion of the County comprised within the Parishes of

MONKSTOWN, KILL-OF-THE-GRANGE, DALKEY, KILLINEY, TULLY, STILLORGAN, AND KILMACUD

FRANCIS ELRINGTON BALL

Published by Left of Brain Books

Copyright © 2021 Left of Brain Books

ISBN 978-1-396-32198-6

First Edition

All rights reserved. No part of this publication may be reproduced, distributed, or transmitted in any form or by any means, including photocopying, recording, or other electronic or mechanical methods, without the prior written permission of the publisher, except in the case of brief quotations embodied in critical reviews and certain other noncommercial uses permitted by copyright law. Left of Brain Books is a division of Left of Brain Onboarding Pty Ltd.

Table of Contents

PREFACE TO THE FIRST PART.	1
INTRODUCTION TO THE FIRST PART.	4
AUTHORITIES.	6
PARISH OF MONKSTOWN.	9
The Castle of Monkstown.	9
Seapoint and Templehill.	21
Blackrock.	31
Montpelier and Its Neighbourhood.	34
The Port of Kingstown.	37
Bullock.	43
Ecclesiastical History of Monkstown.	50
PARISH OF KILL-OF-THE-GRANGE.	57
Kill-of-the-Grange and Dean's Grange.	57
Rochestown.	63
Killiney Hill.	67
Ballinclea.	70
Cabinteely.	71
Tipperstown.	74
Newtownpark.	75
Ecclesiastical History.	76
PARISH OF DALKEY.	81
The Town of Dalkey.	81
Dalkey Island.	88
Ecclesiastical History.	93
PARISH OF KILLINEY.	95

Killiney.	95
Loughlinstown.	98
Hackettsland.	107
Kilbogget.	108
Ecclesiastical History.	108
PARISH OF TULLY.	111
Carrickmines Castle.	111
Laughanstown	117
Brenanstown.	118
Kerrymount.	120
Murphystown.	121
Leopardstown.	122
Ecclesiastical History.	125
PARISH OF STILLORGAN.	129
Stillorgan Park.	129
Ecclesiastical History.	145
PARISH OF KILMACUD.	147
Kilmacud.	147
Ecclesiastical History.	149

PREFACE TO THE FIRST PART.

SOME explanation is, I feel, needed of the reasons which have led me to attempt a task which has already been performed with credit by another author.

The undertaking of this work has been due to no feeling of confidence that John D'Alton's "History of the County Dublin," so far as his general treatment of the subject is concerned, could be improved upon. It has originated in a consideration of the quantity of material which has been made available since my predecessor wrote, and of the inadequate space allotted by him to the annals of some of the districts.

My aim has been to interest the ordinary reader, rather than the specialist, who can best obtain his information from original authorities, and for this reason I have avoided technical descriptions and details. As the events of the last hundred years would have occupied an undue proportion of the history I have practically confined its scope to the conclusion of the eighteenth century.

The parish, which I have chosen as the geographical unit, has been selected because in England it has been found the most convenient division for local history, and though Irish parishes are sadly wanting in the wealth of historical material which those of England afford, still they rival them in early origin, and in most cases possess remains of the primitive church in which their inhabitants at one time united in common worship.

Much of the information, which this part contains, has been contributed to the proceedings of the Royal Society of Antiquaries of Ireland in two papers read by the late Professor Stokes on "The Antiquities from Kingstown to Dublin," and in five papers of my own entitled, "Stillorgan Park and its History," "Some Residents of Monkstown in the Eighteenth Century," "Monkstown Castle and its History," "Loughlinstown and its History," and "The Castle of Carrickmines and its History." For the opportunity thus given me of revising my work, and for kindly sympathy as well as assistance, my thanks are due, and are most gratefully given to my brother fellows and members.

It would be impossible for me to mention all the friends to whom I am indebted for encouragement and help, but there are some to whom I must express in particular my acknowledgments. To one who is no longer with us, my valued friend, Professor George T. Stokes, I owe my introduction to archaeology, and the conception of this history. Mr. James Mills, the Deputy Keeper of the Records in Ireland, has contributed largely to the completeness of this part by his suggestions and acquaintance with the district of which it treats. With generosity all their own, the Rev. William Reynell has ever placed at my service the result of his extensive original research, and Mr. C. Litton Falkiner has given me the benefit of his wide knowledge of Irish historical literature. To Mr. Tenison Groves, whose mastery of Irish records is only equalled by his industry, I am indebted for transcripts of many of the documents of which I have made use. And amongst others who have assisted me I cannot omit Captain W. H. Rotheram, R.E., Dr. P. W. Joyce, Mr. Robert Cochrane, Mr. M. J. M'Enery, Mr. James Talbot Power, Major Herbert W. Domvile, Mr. William P. Geoghegan, Sir Arthur Vicars, Mr. G. D. Burtchaell, and, last but not least, Mr. Alfred de Burgh and the assistants in the library of Trinity College, Dublin, Mr. T. W. Lyster and the assistants in the National Library of Ireland, Mr. J. J. M'Sweeney and the assistants in the library of the Royal Irish Academy, and the librarians and assistants of the Bodleian, and of the British Museum.

The Controller of His Majesty's Stationery Office has given me permission to make use of the Ordnance Map for the purposes of the frontispiece; and the blocks from which some of the illustrations have been taken have been lent me by the Council of the Royal Society of Antiquaries of Ireland.

F. ELRINGTON BALL.

Dublin,
January, 1902.

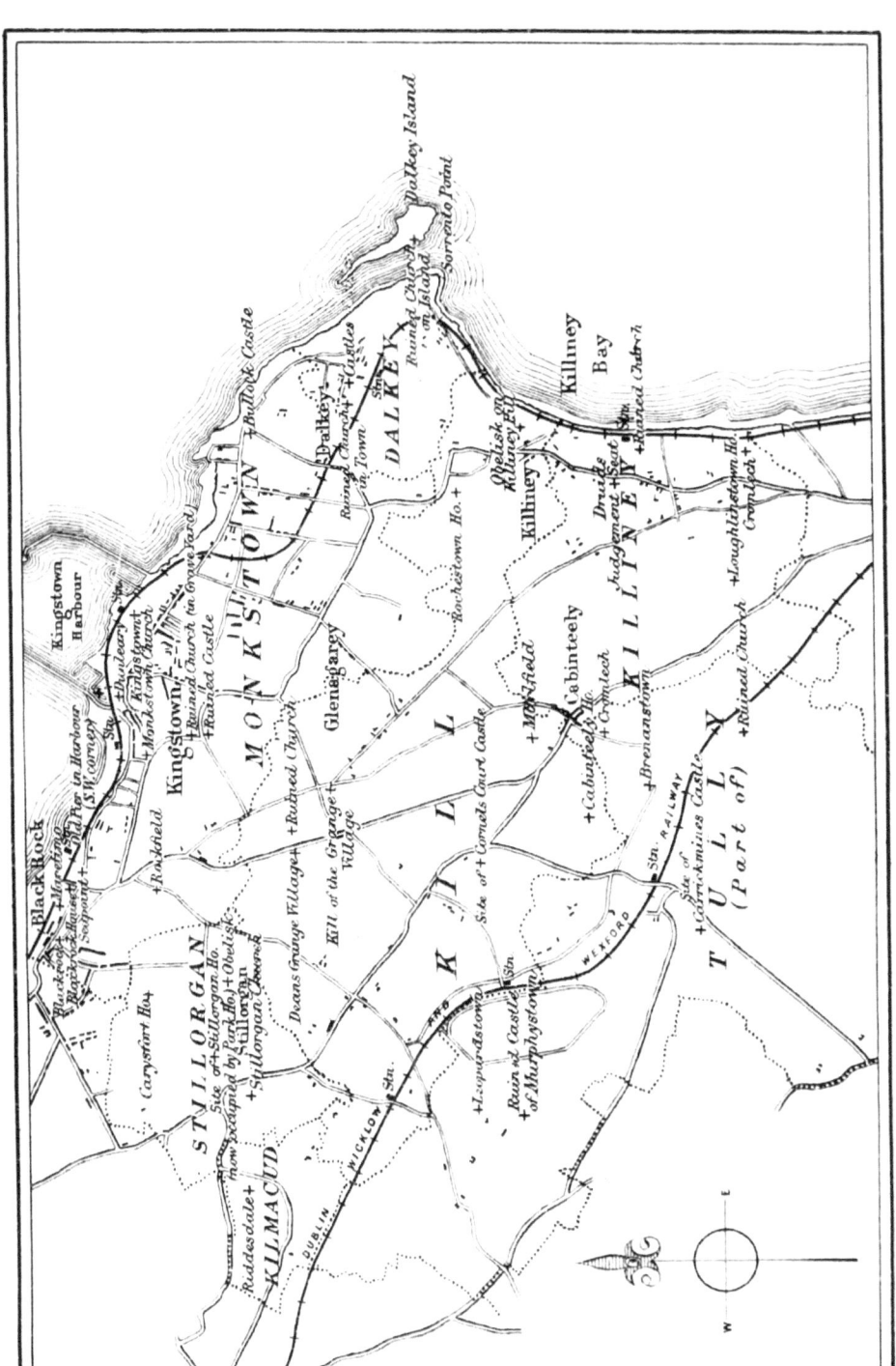

INTRODUCTION TO THE FIRST PART.

THE parishes, which have been grouped in the present part of this history, were closely connected in past times. In the eighteenth century they were united for ecclesiastical purposes under the Established Church, and in the mediæval ages they were, with the exception of Kilmacud, under the spiritual care of the Priory of the Holy Trinity, which, on the dissolution of the religious houses by Henry VIII, became the Cathedral establishment of the Church of the Holy Trinity, commonly called Christ Church. Owing to the modern divisions for the purposes of religious ministration not following the same line, the extent of the original parishes is little known to the present inhabitants; but the latter are still used for civil purposes, and will be found clearly defined on the maps of the Ordnance Survey. They lie to the south-east of the City of Dublin, in the barony of Rathdown, between the sea and the Dublin Mountains, and extend along the coast from Blackrock to Shanganagh, having for their western boundaries the parishes of Taney, Kilgobbin, and Kilternan, and containing the populous townships of Kingstown, Dalkey, and Killiney, and more than half of the township of Blackrock.

This history treats of the district in circumstances and appearance widely different from those with which we are, familiar, and impressions gained merely from knowledge of the present condition of the neighbourhood of Dublin are likely to be very misleading. When our history opens the southern part of the County Dublin formed part of the territory of the people of Cualann, which included also the eastern part of the County Wicklow, and was a wild tract of country covered with woods, bogs, and stony pastures. Amidst the woods here and there clusters of the dwellings of the period—small round houses made of mud and wattles—were to be seen; while on Dalkey Island and at Dunleary stood stone or earthern fortifications, known as duns, to protect the territory from foreign invasion.

In mediæval ages, when the lands for the most part belonged to monastic owners, the district covered by these parishes was rescued from its primeval barrenness, tilled and cultivated, but owing to the frequent incursions of the Irish tribes by whom the Wicklow Mountains were inhabited, this was done by men with one hand on the spear and the other on the plough. The population was very small, and the occupation of the lands was only possible through the erection of strongly-fortified castles, in which the inhabitants took refuge when necessity arose.

But even coming down to the eighteenth century we find the difference great between the district then and at the present time. The whole sea border is now built over with a succession of streets, terraces, and villas, hardly a site being unoccupied by a house. A century and a-half ago the population of the seven parishes was returned as 2,128, while in 1891 it exceeded 30,000. Kingstown was represented by a small village called Dunleary; Dalkey a place of importance in mediæval times, comprised, besides the ruins of its former prosperity, only one or two houses and a few cabins; and Killiney was a seaside hamlet. Two churches, those of Monkstown and Stillorgan, sufficed for the members of the Established Church, and one was all the Roman Catholic Church was known to possess. Fields of corn waved where roads and houses are now to be seen and the only habitations, besides country residences, comparatively few in number, belonging to Dublin citizens, were those of persons deriving their livelihood from farming or fishing.

AUTHORITIES.

The authorities whose titles have been condensed, and the places of preservation of manuscripts, are as follows:—

Journal R. S. A. I. refers to the Journals of the Kilkenny Archæological Society of the Historical and Archæological Society of Ireland, and of the Royal Society of Antiquaries of Ireland, following the consecutive numbering of the Volumes.

Chartularies of St. Mary's Abbey refers to "Chartularies of St. Mary's Abbey, Dublin," edited by Sir John Gilbert in the Rolls Series.

Fiants refers to the Calendars of Fiants in the 7th to the 22nd Reports of the Deputy Keeper of the Records in Ireland.

Christ Church Deeds refers to the Calendar of Christ Church Deeds in the 20th to the 26th Reports of the Deputy Keeper of the Records in Ireland, and to a MS. Calendar preserved in the Public Record Office of Ireland.

Patent and Close Rolls refers to "Rotulorum Patentium et Clausorum Cancellariæ Hiberniæ Caleudarium," vol. i., part i.

Chancery Inquisitions refers to "Inquisitionum in Officio Rotulorum Cancellariæ Hiberniæ Asservartum Repertorium," vol. i., under Co. Dublin.

Fleetwood's Survey refers to "A Survey of the Half Barony of Rathdown," made by order of Lord Deputy Fleetwood; printed in Lodge's "Desiderata Curiosa Hibernica," vol. ii., p. 529.

Archbishop Bulkeley's Report refers to "A Report on the Diocese of Dublin," by Archbishop Bulkeley, printed in *The Irish Ecclesiastical Record*, vol. v., pp. 145-166.

The Down Survey Maps, Hearth Money Roll, Subsidy Rolls, Certificates for Adventurers and Soldiers, Rolls of Innocents, Exchequer Inquisitions (see under Co. Dublin), Book of Postings and Sale, Regal Visitation of 1615, Commission of Grace, Religious Returns of 1766, Wills and Grants are preserved in the Public Record Office of Ireland.

Cooper's Note Book refers to MSS. of Austin Cooper, F.S.A., in possession of the late Mr. Austin Damer Cooper.

Depositions of 1641 are preserved in the Library of Trinity College, Dublin.

Census of 1659 is preserved in the Royal Irish Academy.

Carte Papers are preserved in the Bodleian Library, Oxford.

Monkstown Castle in 1820.
From a Plate drawn by George Petrie in Cromwell's "Excursions through Ireland"

PARISH OF MONKSTOWN.

(Formerly called Carrickbrennan—i.e., Brennan's Rock.)

The Parish of Monkstown is shown on the Down Survey, which was made in 1657, as consisting of the Townlands of Mounekstowne, Newtowne of ye Strand, and Bullock.

Mounekstowne is now represented by the Townlands of Dunleary (*i.e.,* Leaghaire's Dun), Glasthule (*i.e.,* Glas Tuathail, or Toole's Streamlet), Glenageary (*i.e.,* Glleann na geaerach, or the Glen of the Sheep), Honeypark, Lansville, Monkstown, Monkstown Castle Farm, Monkstown House Farm, Mountashton, and Thomastown.

Newtowne is represented by Montpelier, Newtown Blackrock, Newtown Castle Byrne, Rockfield, Seapoint or Templehill, and Stradbrook. Bullock is unaltered.

The objects of archæological interest in the parish are the remains of Bullock Castle, Monkstown Castle, and the ruined Church of Monkstown.

THE CASTLE OF MONKSTOWN.

THE history of the district comprised within the parish of Monkstown centres round the castle, remains of which are to be seen in the grounds of the modern house to which the designation of castle has been attached. As originally constructed, the Castle of Monkstown was a massive pile of mediæval buildings. It consisted of a mansion house, standing in a courtyard, some acres in extent, enclosed by high walls and guarded by three strong towers. Of these buildings only portions of the gate tower and of the mansion house remain; of the former, which was two storeys in height, the arched entrance and a chamber are standing, and of the latter a lofty shell without floors[1]. But, as the

---

[1] "The Lesser Castles of the Country Dublin," by E. R. M'C. Dix., in *The Irish Builder* for 1898, p. 115.

accompanying picture shows, the ruins were a century ago much more complete, and indicated the great size as well as strength of the fortress.

Monkstown Castle in 1803.

The Castle, which was probably built in the twelfth or thirteenth century, was erected by the monks of the Abbey of the Blessed Virgin Mary, near Dublin. This Abbey, whose site is marked by the alley off Capel-street, which bears its name[2], stood outside the walls of ancient Dublin, on the northern bank of the River Liffey, in what was then a rural district known as the meadow of herbs, and had been founded before the Anglo-Norman Conquest. Amongst the lands with which it had been endowed were those of Carrickbrennan, now forming the greater part of the civil parish of Monkstown, and including the lands on which Kingstown, Glenageary, and

---

[2] See *Journal R.S.A.I.*, vol. xxi., p. 271.

Bullock are built. These were probably given to the Abbey by one of its founders, a Celtic chief called MacGillamocholmog, who held sway over the southern portion of the County Dublin, and were in possession of the monks when the Anglo-Norman invasion took place[3]. The Conquest did not directly make any alteration in the ownership, as with lands dedicated to the Church Henry II. did not interfere when distributing his newly-acquired territory amongst the invaders; but it had indirectly the effect of producing a change of proprietors. One of the first results of the Conquest was to transform the Celtic monasteries into Anglo-Norman ones, and a new race of monks supplanted the former occupants. St. Mary's Abbey had been affiliated early in the twelfth century to the Cistercian Order, and in its case fresh tenants were supplied by the great Cistercian House of Buildwas, in Shropshire[4], under whose cure and disposition it was placed.

These monks brought with them new ideas and acquirements. Chief amongst their attainments was a knowledge of agriculture. Monasteries in England were famous for their system of tillage; and the White Monks, as the members of the Cistercian Order were called, on account of the colour of their clothing, were remarkable for their life of unintermitting toil spent more in the field than in the cloister. Soon the lands of Carrickbrennan, as well as those round the Abbey on the Liffey, became subject to the plough; portion was retained in the hands of the monks themselves, and the remainder was let to tenants who, in most cases, were bound to render a certain amount of labour, either in person or by deputy, on the home farm. To their skill in agriculture the new monks joined a knowledge of fishing—an industry which the Cistercian Order, whose lands usually bordered on the sea or rivers, did much to promote, and under their auspices an extensive fishery grew up at Bullock.

After the Conquest, many of the Celtic inhabitants of the lands round Dublin remained as the hewers of wood and drawers of water, but some took refuge in the fastnesses of the Wicklow Mountains. From thence the latter made unceasing raids on the property of the colonists, carrying off their cattle, and burning and devastating their lands. The monks soon perceived that their

---

[3] "The Norman Settlement in Leinster," by James Mill, in *Journal R.S.A.I.*, vol. xxiv., p. 161.

[4] See Walcott's "Four Minsters round the Wrekin" and Anderson's "History and Antiquities of Shropshire."

possessions were only to be held by force of arms, and, for their defence, commenced the erection of the Castles of Monkstown and Bullock—the former to protect their farm, the latter their fishery. As we have seen, Monkstown Castle was provided with a large courtyard, known then as a bawn, and into this, when warning was given by watchers stationed on the Dublin Mountains that an incursion was imminent, the inhabitants gathered with their flocks and herds, and the hillsmen descended on the plain to find it swept of every living thing, and to hear the lowing cattle and the bleating sheep proclaiming their safety from within the Castle bawn.

Of the history of Monkstown during the three centuries of its occupation by monastic owners, there is little information. At the close of the thirteenth century, its lands were returned in a taxation of the diocese of Dublin as worthless, owing to the state of war to which they were subject, and a few years later the Abbey was obliged to negotiate with the Irish enemies of the King for the restitution of goods carried away from its grange. A determined effort appears to have been made about the middle of the, fourteenth century to resist the incursions of the tribes. A militia force was raised, to which the Abbey undertook to contribute in respect of Monkstown two heavy and six light horsemen, and a permanent garrison was maintained at Bray, though even then the Irish at times got the upper hand. As regards the relations between the Abbey and its tenants at Monkstown, the only recorded event is that in the fifteenth century, owing to "felonies, extortions, and contempts" committed by the abbot and his monks, the Abbey was deprived for a year of its manorial jurisdiction.

Meanwhile the Abbey on the Liffey had become a place of national importance and convenience. Inns were then unknown in Ireland, and, if it had not been for the hospitable Cistercian monks, travellers would have been without shelter in Dublin. But in St. Mary's Abbey, and doubtless also in its castles at Monkstown and Bullock, which were on the direct road from Dalkey, the Kingstown of the period, they were always sure of accommodation and of welcome. When, therefore, the order came from Henry VIII. for the dissolution of the Irish religious houses, the Lord Deputy urged that St. Mary's Abbey should be allowed to stand, on account of its being the resort of all persons of position coming from England, and the monks set forth that the Abbey existed for the benefit of others than their community. It was, however, to no purpose; St. Mary's Abbey, in common with nearly all Irish monasteries, was demolished, and its possessions became the property of the Crown[5].

A few years after the suppression of the Abbey, which took place towards the close of the year 1539, the Castle of Monkstown, together with its lands (excepting those of Bullock), was granted by Henry VIII. to the Right Honourable Sir John Travers, Master of the Ordnance in Ireland, and a Groom of the Chamber to the King. The lands were described in the inquisitions under the denominations of the town and the grange. The former, which was by far the largest, was let to tenants, who occupied four houses and thirteen cottages, and paid rent in money and kind, and the latter, on which the Castle stood, had been the home farm of the monks, and was occupied by their bailiff. For the next twenty years, until his death, Travers used the Castle as his country seat and principal residence. During the greater part of that period he held a chief place amongst the military adventurers to whom the destinies of Ireland were committed in the sixteenth century. In England he had been a person of comparative obscurity, but he possessed capacity, interest, and adaptability—qualities which then brought a man to the front in Ireland, and enabled him to amass a large fortune. Besides, he had the advantage of previous acquaintance with the country, in which he had been born, and a knowledge of the Celtic language, together with an open and generous character, which commended him to those with whom he was brought in contact, and a fine physique, which enabled him to stand the hardships, unparalleled in their severity, of campaigning in Ireland.

We find him first residing at Oxford, where he was a Commissioner of Taxation, then acting as a gentleman at large in the household of Henry VIII.'s natural son, the Duke of Richmond, when he was given a grant of the fishing of the River Bann, and a license to export wool from Ireland, and, after the Dukes untimely death, serving in the Army—taking part in the suppression of the rising under Aske, in Yorkshire, and being present as a spectator at military operations in the Netherlands. He had interest at Court through the Earl of Southampton, then Lord Admiral, and one of the most powerful

---

[5] "Chartularies of St. Mary's Abbey;" Bagwell's "Ireland under the Tudors," vol. i., p. 318; Christ Church Deeds, No. 150; Patent and Close Rolls, pp. 206, 210, 262.

personages in England, whose kinsman and secretary his sister had married, and on his return from abroad the King, who remembered him as one who had been in attendance on his favourite son, appointed him Groom of his Chamber and Serjeant of his Tents, and made use of his military knowledge in the construction of defence works on the Thames. At the time of the dissolution of the Irish religious houses the Army was reduced to a perilously low condition, and it was determined to reinforce it. The opportunity was a tempting one to a man like Travers, and he secured for himself the command of the Artillery, then sent over. He had not been long in Ireland before he established a high reputation for himself as a good soldier, both in the field and in the barrack, and not less as a sagacious adviser in the Council, on which he had been given a seat. In the latter capacity, as suited the policy of the time, he was a strong advocate of firm government by military force if necessary, as well as of the establishment of the Protestant religion, and of the abolition of Irish customs, usages, and laws.

After some years, during which his time was completely absorbed by his duties, which entailed expeditions to every part of the country, and the organisation of an efficient army, his reward came. On his arrival he had been given St. Mary's Abbey as a storehouse for the ordnance, and as a residence for himself, in which he might exercise the hospitality becoming his position. To this was added a grant of the Castle and lands of Monkstown, and a number of castles and great extent of lands in various parts of the country. From being comparatively poor, Travers became a man of wealth, and his social position was raised by the honour of knighthood, which was conferred upon him. Holding such views as he did he found no difficulty in accommodating himself to the changes made by the accession of Edward VI., and the Lord Deputies under that monarch all expressed their satisfaction with him. Sir Edward Bellingham found in him a soldier after his own heart, and Sir James Croft, who stayed at Monkstown on at least one occasion, had in him a willing assistant in his efforts to introduce the Protestant liturgy. The transition from the rule of Edward to that of Mary cannot have been so congenial, and Travers can only have retained his office by some sacrifice of his principles. His age prevented his taking as active a part as he had formerly done in affairs of State, and towards the close of this reign he had to relinquish the duties of his office to another, being granted, on his retirement, a pension and a retinue of six horsemen and six musketeers. He survived for four years after Elizabeth's accession, his death taking place in 1562[6].

His place at Monkstown was taken by James Eustace, eldest son of the second Viscount Baltinglas, who, on account of his share in the Desmond Rebellion after he had succeeded to his father's titles, plays a prominent part in the Elizabethan history of Ireland. Eustace's possession of Monkstown was in right of his wife, who was a granddaughter of Sir John Travers. No children appear to have survived the latter, who was twice married, and his property on his death passed to the children of a son called Henry, who had pre-deceased him. This son had made an alliance with one of the great families of the Pale by his marriage to Gennet Preston, daughter of Jenico, third Viscount Gormanston, and left by her, who married, as her second husband, Robert Pipho, ancestor of the Marquess of Waterford, two daughters, Mary, who married James Eustace, and Katherine, who married John Cheevers, of Macetown, in the County Meath. Eustace after his marriage had gone to London to perfect his education and, owing to legal informalities in the transfer of Travers' property to him and his wife, it was seized by the Crown. In 1565 Sir Henry Sidney, the father of the renowned Sir Philip Sidney, on his arrival as Lord Deputy, spent a night at Monkstown on his way from Dalkey to Dublin, and the Castle was possibly then occupied under the Crown by one of the Barnewall family. It was, however, restored to Eustace, then Viscount Baltinglas, before he openly joined the Desmond Rebellion. There meetings of his confederates were frequently held, and there Eustace narrowly escaped being taken prisoner. After his attainder in 1580 his kinsman, the Earl of Kildare, sought to obtain from the Crown the custody of the Castle, but it was given to the Vice-Treasurer, Sir Henry Wallop, ancestor of the Earls of Portsmouth. Wallop's occupation was, however, of short duration, for, in spite of his opposition, it was restored to the Viscountess Baltinglas, in common with all the property she had brought to her husband[7].

---

[6] "Letters and Papers of the reign of Henry VIII.," 1523-1542; "State Papers, Henry VIII.," vol. iii.; "Calendar of State Papers, Ireland," 1509-1573; Fiants; "Pedigree of the Devonshire Family of Travers," by S. Smith Travers, edited by R. J. Hone and F. B. Falkiner.

[7] "Dictionary of National Biography," vol. xviii., p. 51; Funeral Entries in Ulster's Office; Harris' "History of Dublin," p. 35; "Calendar of State Papers. Ireland," 1509-1573, 1574-1585; Fiant, Elizabeth, No. 465; "Calendar of Carew State Papers," 1575-1588.

A few years later Sir Gerald Aylmer, of Donadea, in the County Kildare, whose descendants still hold the baronetcy conferred on him by James I., came into possession of the Castle, through his marriage to the Viscountess Baltinglas after the death of the Viscount in Spain, where he had taken refuge. Aylmer had not been, so far as was known, implicated in the Desmond Rebellion, but his sympathies undoubtedly lay with those who were concerned in it, and his adherence to the Roman Catholic faith and efforts to secure the amelioration of the condition of his co-religionists, led more than once to his imprisonment. Subsequently, however, notwithstanding his convictions, which he appears to have held through life, he received from Elizabeth the honour of knighthood, afterwards merged in the hereditary title of baronet, of which he was one of the first recipients[8].

After the death of his wife in 1610, the Castle and lands passed from Aylmer's possession into that of his wife's nephew. Henry Cheevers, her sister's second son. The latter married a daughter of his neighbour, Sir Richard Fitzwilliam, ancestor in the female line of the Earls of Pembroke, whose Castle at Merrion was the only dwelling of importance between Monkstown and Dublin, and passed an uneventful life in the Castle. To him succeeded, on his death in 1640, his son, Walter Cheevers, who was residing in the Castle when the Commonwealth was established. He appears to have taken no part in the stirring events of the time, but, as a Roman Catholic, he was not long left undisturbed. The Castle was a tempting residence for one of the authorities of the Parliament, and commanding as it did the landing-place for the men-of-war which lay in the roads, now occupied by Kingstown Harbour, it was of importance that it should be in the hands of one trusted by the Government. Cheevers was, therefore, amongst the first who were ordered to transplant into Connaught, although, from the steps taken to give him a suitable dwelling and ample lands there, it is evident that the only cause of complaint against him was his religion, and in the depth of the winter of 1653, he received command to vacate his ancestral home, and with his wife, a daughter of Viscount Netterville, and his five children, the eldest being only seven years of age, to find a new one in the wilds of the West of Ireland. His

---

[8] "Donadea and the Aylmer Family," by Rev. Canon Sherlock in *Journal of the County Kildare Archæological Society*, vol. iii., p. 169: "Calendar of State Papers. Ireland," 1588-1592; "The Description of Ireland in 1598," edited by Rev. Edmund Hogan, p. 37.

circumstances were not too flourishing, but he was surrounded by the usual crowd of retainers, and six men and four women servants accompanied their master. Also four tenants elected to share their landlord's fortunes, and the progress of so great a company, with their horses, cattle, sheep, pigs, and goods, across Ireland in winter must have been attended with loss, as well as hardship[9].

An owner for the Castle was forthcoming in the person of Lieutenant General Edmund Ludlow, one of the best known of the regicides, who was then Commander of the Horse in Ireland, and one of the commissioners for its government, and who probably had something to do with Cheevers' eviction. The Castle was then in want of repair, but this Ludlow, who lost no opportunity of acquiring wealth—even making fortune the first consideration in his choice of a wife—soon effected, and caused gardens and pleasure grounds to be laid out, in which he delighted to walk. His establishment was in keeping with his residence; no one surpassed him in hospitality, and twenty horses stood ready for service in his stables. The breeding of horses, of black cattle, and of sheep, amused him in his leisure hours, and probably he had at times opportunity of exercising his love for hunting—a sport to which he was passionately devoted. But his enjoyment of his newly-acquired possessions was brief. He strongly disapproved of Cromwell's assumption of regal power, and when the Lord Protectors son, Henry, came over to feel his way before his appointment as Lord Lieutenant of Ireland. Ludlow, who met him at Dunleary with his coach, and entertained him at the Castle, both on his arrival and departure, disclosed to him while walking in the Castle garden his dissatisfaction with the step his father had taken. From that time Ludlow's position in the Government became untenable. He desired to go to England, but Cromwell preferred his remaining in Ireland, and it was at last without Cromwell's leave that he set sail on a stormy day in October, 1655, for England, accompanied to the boat by a vast crowd of his neighbours, with whom he was most popular. After four years' absence, on the recall of the Long Parliament, Ludlow returned to Ireland invested with all his former power, and for a few months resided again

---

[9] "Lodge's Peerage of Ireland," edited by Mervyn Archdall, vol. vii., p. 58, vol. iv., p. 315; Will of Henry Cheevers; Archbishop Bulkeley's Report; Prendergast's "Cromwellian Settlement," 2nd edition, p. 176.

at the Castle, which had been looked after for him by his brother-in-law, Colonel Kempston. He then went over to London; while he was there the Army began to waver in their allegiance to the Parliament, and on his hurrying back to Ireland his landing was successfully opposed. Ludlow foresaw what was coming, and before the Restoration, sent orders to his bailiff to sell his stock, valued at £1.500, but through negligence or treachery on the part of his servant there was delay in the execution of his order, and all his possessions were seized by the Army for the Crown[10].

Some months after the Restoration, in November, 1660, Walter Cheevers was restored to his estates. So far as Monkstown was concerned, it was probably much improved, the Castle (which was one of the largest dwellings in the County Dublin, and contained six chimneys, a most unusual number) was in excellent repair, as well as a corn mill which stood near to it, and the population of the lands was returned as eleven English and fifty-three Irish, of whom fifteen besides Cheevers were householders[11].

In the latter part of the seventeenth century the Castle and lands came into the possession of the Most Rev. Michael Boyle[12] who held, in addition to the See of Armagh, the Chancellorship of Ireland, a combination of ecclesiastical and legal offices common in earlier times, but last permitted in his case, and the ownership of the soil still remains in possession of his descendants, now represented by Lords Longford and De Vesci[13]. A description of the Castle one hundred years later shows that it must have been modernised and enlarged after Ludlow's time. These improvements were probably effected by Archbishop Boyle's eldest son, Viscount Blessington, whose son, the second and last Viscount Blessington, and son-in-law, Viscount Mountjoy, subsequently held the lands. Cheevers' death took place in 1678, and the,

---

[10] "Memoirs of Edmund Ludlow," edited by C. H. Firth; Fleetwood's Survey; Down Survey.

[11] "Carte Papers;" Census of 1659; Hearth Money Roll; Certificates for Adventurers and Soldiers, xiii., 45.

[12] See notice of Archbishop Boyle and authorities quoted in "Some Notes on the Irish Judiciary in the reign of Charles II." in *Journal of the Cork Archæological and Historical Society*, 2nd Ser., vol. vii., p. 36.

[13] "Descent of the Monkstown Estate," by R. S. Longworth-Dames, in Journal *R.S.A.I.*, vol. xxiii., p. 430; Grant under Commission of Grace.

marriage of a connection of Lord Blessington's in 1686, at Monkstown, indicates that the Castle was then one of his residences[14].

Amongst other persons residing at Monkstown at that time were Mr. Michael Hare, who died in 1685, and was buried in St. Patrick's Cathedral, and Mr. Edward Corker, some time M.P. for Ratoath, and son-in-law of Sir Daniel Bellingham, the first Lord Mayor of Dublin. About the time of the latter's death, in 1702, the Honourable Anthony Upton, a kinsman of the Uptons of Antrim, now ennobled under the title of Templetown, who had just been appointed a judge of the Court of Common Pleas, came to live at Monkstown. His residence there has been commemorated by a famous ecclesiastical lawyer and writer of that period, Dr. William King, who was then Judge of the Irish Admiralty Court and Vicar-General of Armagh, in a poem entitled "Mully of Mountown." It describes a discussion between the Judge's servants—Peggy, the nymph of Mountown, David, a sprightly swain, who drove the Judge's coach, and Robin of Derbyshire, the surly herd—as to the fate of the cow Mully—whether she was to be devoted to the dairy or to the butcher—and tells of the garden produce and refreshing beverages for which Monkstown was renowned. Upton's death did not take place till 1718, when he terminated his life with his own hand, but he had given up his house at Monkstown before that time, on his removal from the Bench on the accession of George I., and was then living in London[15].

In the middle of the eighteenth century we find at Monkstown Dr. Robert Roberts, an eminent Doctor of Laws, and M.P. for the Borough of Dungarvan, who died in 1758, when his extensive library was sold, and subsequently Mr. Robert Elrington, a West Indian merchant, and probably a descendant of the well-known Dublin actor, Thomas Elrington[16]. About the same time a house was built on the opposite side of the road from the

---

[14] Viscount Blessington's eldest daughter married Sir John Dillon, and in 1686 Captain William Blayney, afterwards 6th Baron Blayney, married in Monkstown Church the widow of Arthur Dillon, of Lismullen. Monkstown Parish Register.

[15] Adams' "History of Santry," p. 35; "Works of William King. LL.D" vol. i., p. xviii., vol. iii., p. 203; Foster's "Alumnii Oxonienses;" "Lincoln's Inn Admissions;" "Black Book of Lincoln's Inn;" Smyth's "Law Officers of Ireland;" Lodge's "Peerage of Ireland," edited by Mervyn Archdall, vol. vii., p. 155.

[16] *Pue's Occurrences*, vol. Iv., No. 12: Religious Return of 1766; Monkstown Parish Register; Prerogative Grant, Robert Elrington.

Castle, where the gate lodge of Monkstown Park now stands, by the Right Honourable Charles Jones, fifth Viscount Ranelagh, who had claimed as a descendant of the first Viscount, the title which had lain dormant from the death of his kinsman, the notorious Earl of Ranelagh. He took a prominent part in the political affairs of his time as Chairman of Committees in the Irish House of Lords, and, in spite of his support of the English Government, to which he was indebted for a pension, was a most popular nobleman. During his long residence in Monkstown, where he lived until his death, in 1797, he was a constant attendant at the vestries, and was instrumental in establishing an association for the repression of the footpads, with whom the roads swarmed[17]. His house was pulled down in 1843, on the erection in its grounds of the one known as Monkstown Park, by Mr. Charles Haliday, whose memory will ever be preserved in his noble collection of pamphlets and books relating to Ireland, now in the possession of the Royal Irish Academy[18].

The Castle was, in 1780, advertised to be sold, and was then visited by one of the best Irish antiquaries of that day—Mr. Austin Cooper, F.S.A.[19]. The buildings at that time consisted of two square castles with turrets, a high tower, and a house in the Gothic style, which stood behind the castles. The house is described in the advertisement, which is written in the most high-flown language, as the second best in the county on the south side of the Liffey. It was three storeys in height, and comprised numerous apartments, including a saloon, library, gallery, and chapel. The tower, which was 91 feet high, afforded a most extensive prospect. There were numerous offices, and the gardens, of which a glowing account is given, contained ice-houses, ferneries, and greenhouses[20]. It was subsequently taken by Councillor O'Neill, M.P. for Clonakilty, and at the termination of his tenancy appears to have been allowed to fall into ruin. A proposal was made by Mr. James

---

[17] Cokayne's "Complete Peerage:" Will of 5th Viscount Ranelagh: " Lansdowne Papers," British Museum Add. MS, 24137, ii., 59, 72, 90: Blacker's "Sketches of Booterstown," p. 174; *Dublin Chronicle.* 1787-1788, p. 568.

[18] "The Scandinavian Kingdom of Ireland," by Charles Holiday; edited, with life of the author, by John P. Prendergast, p. xiv.

[19] See notice of Austin Cooper's life, by E. R. M'C. Dix, in *The Irish Builder* for 1897, p. 103.

[20] Cooper's Note Book; *Saunder's Newsletter,* Oct. 4, 1788.

Pim, in 1838, to the Royal Zoological Society of Ireland, to transfer their collection to the grounds of the Castle, but, while acknowledging his liberal and scientific spirit, the Council did not think that they were at liberty to entertain it[21].

SEAPOINT AND TEMPLEHILL.

(Formerly called Newtown on the Strand, or Newtown Castle Byrne.)

THE lands on which Seapoint and Templehill now stand formed at the time of the Norman Conquest portion of those of Stillorgan, and were known as Argortin, or the Tillage-Lands. At the beginning of the thirteenth century they were given, as a solemn religious offering, by Raymond Carew, the Anglo-Norman owner of Stillorgan, to St. Mary's Abbey, and, when added to its lands of Carrickbrennan, completed the contents of the civil parish of Monkstown. On the dissolution of the Abbey, in 1539, the lands of Newtown, as they were then called, contained a small castle house, besides other dwellings, and were held by a tenant called John Moran. They were granted by the Crown to Sir John Travers at the same time as those of Monkstown, and, like the latter, were subsequently held by Viscount Baltinglas, Sir Gerald Aylmer, the Cheevers family, and Edmund Ludlow. The tithes, which had also belonged to the Abbey, were retained by the Crown, and in the sixteenth century were leased to, amongst others, James Stanyhurst, Speaker of the House of Commons, and Recorder of Dublin, the father of the well-known historian, and to Thomas, Earl of Ossory, the lands being then described as Newtown on the Strand, or Newtown-juxta-Mare. In the time of the Commonwealth the Castle, which was slated, was in good repair, and the population was returned as two English and twelve Irish, of whom six were householders. After the Restoration the lands of Newtown were restored, together with those of Monkstown, to Walter Cheevers, and on his death, in 1678, passed to the Byrne family, through the marriage of his only surviving child to John Byrne, of whom we shall hear more under Cabinteely.[22]

---

[21] "Postchaise Companion;" Minutes of Council of the Royal Zoological Society.
[22] "Chartularies of St. Mary's Abbey," vol. i., p. 111, vol. ii., p. 63; Fiant Henry VIII., No. 460; Elizabeth, Nos. 2239, 2960, 3146; Fleetwood's Survey; Down Survey; Census of 1659.

A View of Blackrock and its Neighbourhood in 1744. *(From an engraving drawn by William Jones).*

1. The Salt House. 2. The Black Rocks. 3. Bathing Places. 4. Houses of Entertainment. 5. Lime-Kiln. 6. Newtown-Castle-Byrne. 7. Rocks front of Dunleary. 8. "Dunleary Rocks in the Sea." 9. Lord Allen's Park at Stillorgan. 10. Mount Mapas. 11. Mapas' Obelisk. 12. Sugar Loaf Mountain. 13. Bray Head. 14. Ships. 15. "The Three Sugar Leaves."

In the early part of the eighteenth century, Newtown Castle Byrne, as it was then called, after the owner of the soil, was a pleasure resort for the citizens of Dublin. As the picture shows, a small town, which stood near the site of the railway station, had been built, and in a lease of that period the square of Newtown is mentioned. A large assembly-room, known as the Great Room of Castle Byrne, which was supported by subscribers, who dined together during the summer, was erected, and there, in the year 1749, the Lord Chancellor, Robert Jocelyn, then Lord Newport, and afterwards Viscount Jocelyn, ancestor of the Earls of Roden, while residing at Mount Merrion, dined with the gentlemen of his court, to celebrate, after the manner of that time, the Battle of the Boyne. Some fatalities which occurred at Newtown, indicate that sea bathing was then in vogue, and the drowning in August, 1755, of an attorney with the historic name of Boswell, perhaps deserves record[23].

In the year 1757 a distinguished resident, the Right Honourable Edward Willes, who had been appointed in that year Chief Baron of the Irish Exchequer, came to Newtown. Like many of the Irish judges of his day, he was sent direct from the English Bar to the Irish Bench. He belonged to an ancient Warwickshire family, seated at Newbold Comyn, on the lands of which Leamington is built, and held the offices of Recorder of Coventry, Attorney-General of the Duchy of Lancaster, and the rank of King's Serjeant-Law, when promoted to the Irish judiciary. His success in life has been attributed to his being a cousin of the eminent John Willes, Chief Justice of England, but from letters and papers relating to Ireland, which he has left, it is evident that he was a person of striking individuality, possessed of no ordinary discernment and intellectual ability, and of a character in which honesty of intention was conspicuous. His house at Newtown was called Rockfield, and stood near the site of the old castle in what was known as the Castle Field. He describes its situation in a letter to his intimate friend, the Earl of Warwick. After writing of the bay of Dublin, he tells him that he has taken a thatched cabin upon it, for a summer retreat, overhanging a cliff, as high over the sea as Warwick Castle over the Avon; and goes on to say that out of one of his parlour windows nothing intercepted his view of Warwick but the

---

[23] *Pue's Occurrences*, vol. xl., No. 45; *Dublin Journal*, Nos. 1553, 2329, 2951, 3167.

mountains of Wales, and that out of the other window he had a romantic prospect of mountains, valleys, woods, and country houses, with the little town of Newtown underneath, and the obelisk at Stillorgan, then standing in Lord Allen's deer park, and said to be the truest monument of the kind in proportion and beauty of any on this side of the Alps, in the distance.

Willes suffered much from gout and ague, which were aggravated by the dampness of Ireland and the discomforts judges then suffered on circuit, and nine years after his appointment his health completely broke down, and he retired from the Bench. He sought relief in his native air, but only survived two years, dying at Newbold Comyn in 1768, when in the 66th year of his age. A monument to his memory was erected in Leamington Church, the inscription on which records his many virtues. His eldest son, who took Orders, was educated in Dublin University, where he was always selected while a student to address the Lords Lieutenants in set speeches on their visits to the College, and afterwards, by his classical learning and accomplishments, did credit to his *Alma Mater*[24].

Another resident at Newtown at that time was the Honourable Robert Marshall, one of the judges of the Common Pleas, known to students of Swift as one of the executors of Esther Vanhomrigh. Swift attributed to him responsibility for the publication of the poem of "Cadenus and Vanessa," but certainly, in after years, there was no desire on his part to injure the Dean, and he was active in promoting, after Swift's death, a monument to his memory. He represented Clonmel, of which place he was a native, in Parliament, before his elevation to the Bench, and probably he was one of those grave serjeants-at-law, spoken of by a contemporary writer, who, when they rose to speak in the House near midnight, were as certain though sad harbingers of day as the bird of dawning. Legal talent in Ireland was then not at a high level, and Marshall appears, from his conduct of the claimant's case in the Annesley Peerage suit, to have been at least equal to his fellows. In 1754 he was promoted to the Bench, and occupied a seat in the Common Pleas, until

---

[24] Colvile's "Worthies of Warwickshire," p. 812: "Letters from Chief Baron Willes to the Earl of Warwick," British Museum Add. MS 29252: Historical Manuscripts Commission. Report ii., App., p. 103; Report iii., App. p. 435; Leases in Registry of Deeds Office; Field's "Account of Warwick and Leamington." p. 330; Field's "Memoirs of Rev. Samuel Parr." vol. i., p. 204: *Dublin Journal*, Nos. 3111, 3125, 3182, 3819.

obliged to retire about the same time as Willes, and from the same cause. He continued, however, to reside at Newtown, and died, in 1774, at his residence, which was called Seapoint House. His wife, a descendant through her mother of Sir Abraham Yarner, eminent in the Ireland of the Restoration, both in the practice of medicine and the profession of arms, brought Marshall, it is said, a fortune of £30,000, and he was not destitute himself of private means. They had no children; her fortune passed to her nieces, now represented by Viscount Combermere, and his property to the children of his sister, who had married Thomas Christmas, M.P. for Waterford, now represented by the Duchess of St. Albans. Marshall's remains were interred in Waterford Cathedral with his own family, while his wife, who survived him, was buried with her father, Benjamin Wboley, in Wicklow Churchyard[25].

About the same time Lieutenant-General John Adlercron came to reside at Newtown. He was a member of a Huguenot family, whose ancestors had taken refuge in Dublin at the close of the seventeenth century, and, as Colonel of the 39th Regiment of Foot, had seen much service in India under Lord Clive. In April, 1762, he entertained at dinner, in his house at Newtown, the Lord Lieutenant of the day, the first Earl of Halifax, and there, in July, 1766, after eating a hearty dinner, as we are told, he died of an apoplectic fit. His wife, who belonged also to a Huguenot family and was daughter of an officer, Lieutenant-Colonel John Arabin, survived Adlercron, together with two sons, who both adopted their father's profession, and a daughter, who married Sir Capel Molyneux[26].

Another resident at Newtown at this time was Edward Murphy, the attached friend of the patriotic first Earl of Charlemont. He had accompanied that nobleman as his tutor when, in early days, he made the grand tour, and now dwelt, supported mainly by his patron's bounty, in what he loved to call "his cell hard by ye sable rock," surrounded by the curious and beautiful

---

[25] "Robert Marshall, of Clonmel, Esq." in *Journal of the Cork Historical and Archæological Society*, 2nd Ser., vol. iii., p. 263; Carroll's "Succession of the Clergy of St. Bride's," p. 26; Birkbeck Hill's "Unpublished Letters of Dean Swift," p. 189; Hardy's "Life of Charlemont," vol. i., p. 139.

[26] La Touche's "Register of the French Churches in Dublin" Notes and Queries, 3rd Ser., iv., 383, 460; Wills of the Adlererons: *Exshaw's Magazine* for 1757, p. 608; Lyons' "Grand Juries of the County Westmeath," vol. ii., p. 3; *Pue's Occurrences*, vol. li., No. 54; vol. lix., No. 33; vol. lxiii., No. 6509: *Dublin Journal*. No 2731.

things which he had collected during his travels. Amongst the most remarkable of these was a collection of busts of the Roman Emperors, which were modelled for him from the originals in the Museum at Rome by an Italian artist, who had taken four years to execute the task. These busts he bequeathed to his friend and patron, and they are now in the rooms of the Royal Irish Academy, to which they were presented by the last Earl of Charlemont. Murphy was a good classical scholar, and edited an edition of Lucian, which was long used as a text-book in the University of Dublin, of which he had been a scholar. He was beloved by all who knew him, and attracted round him a host of friends by his charm in conversation and other social gifts, and by the simple and unaffected hospitality of his cell and turret, which ever spared a chop and some fruit to his visitors, and relief to the poor. After many years of suffering, which was lightened, as far as possible, by two wonder-working leeches, the celebrated Dr. Trotter and the sage Dr. Noddy, the former, he says, admirable in fair, the latter in foul weather. Lord Charlemont's devoted hermit breathed his last in September, 1777, while on a visit to the Queen's County, and was buried in Straboe Churchyard, where a monument records his merits[27].

Amongst other contemporary residents at Newtown were Thomas Burroughs, an eminent attorney, connected by marriage with the Nugents, of Clonlost, in the County Westmeath, whose handsome house was surrounded with the choicest fruit trees and flowering shrubs; the Rev. Thomas Heany, the curate in charge of Monkstown Church; and Topham Mitchell, a most charitable and popular gentleman, who died in 1764 from a fall from his horse[28].

Some years later, in 1767, the land on which Temple Hill House stands was bought by Serjeant James Dennis, who was promoted to the Bench, in 1777, as Chief Baron of the Exchequer, and created a peer as Baron Tracton. There he erected the present residence, which was long known as Neptune.

---

[27] "Correspondence of James. 1st Earl of Charlemont," edited by Sir John Gilbert, published by the Historical Manuscripts Commission; Charlemont Papers preserved in the Royal Irish Academy; *Exshaw's Magazine* for 1777. p. 632; *Notes and Queries*, 9th Ser, iii., 261, 373; Proceedings of the Royal Irish Academy. 1866-1869, App., pp. 37, 45; Will of Edward Murphy.

[28] *Dublin Journal*, Nos. 3703, 3868; *Pue's Occurrences*, vol. lxi., Nos. 6283, 6334.

His career as a judge was very short, his death taking place suddenly in his house in Stephen's green, at the corner of Merrion-row, in June, 1782. He was a native of Cork, and his remains were removed to that city for interment in the Cathedral in the vault of the Pigott family, to which his wife belonged[29].

He was succeeded in Neptune by a judge who is much better known, the celebrated John Scott, first Earl of Clonmell, Chief Justice of the King's Bench. Scott was appointed to that high judicial position in 1784, with the title of Baron Earlsfort, and was afterwards advanced to the Viscountcy and Earldom of Clonmell. He is best known through writings in which his memory has been defamed and vilified in every possible way. His character, undoubtedly, was far from perfect, but a recent writer has shown that he was not so infamous as he has been painted, and he was beyond question a man of the first ability, and not without great admirers and friends amongst his contemporaries. At Neptune he made many alterations and improvements, which gave opportunity to his victim, John Magee, owner of the *Dublin Evening Post*, to avenge the tyranny which the Earl, in his judicial capacity, had exercised over him, and which is perhaps the greatest blot on the Earl's career. The land which lay between Neptune and the present Monkstown Church was then open and bare, and in the middle of the eighteenth century it had been the scene of horse-racing, which was generally productive of good sport and close running. It had belonged to Judge Marshall, and was then in the possession of his niece, the widow of Sir William Osborne. In some way Magee secured it, and then proceeded to organise on it a monster fete, at which a pig chase was the principal attraction. The result which Magee desired was attained; immense crowds gathered, and the moment they were let loose, the pigs invaded the gardens of Neptune, followed by the mob in hot pursuit. Before the intruders could be turned out they had overrun the whole place, and the Earl's grounds presented a scene of utter destruction and desolation[30].

---

[29] Cokayne's "Complete Peerage;" "Old Dublin Mansion Houses," by Edward Evans in *The Irish Builder* for 1894, pp. 173, 260; Caulfield's "Annals of St. Fin Barr's Cathedral, Cork," p. 106; Lease in Registry of Deeds Office; *Dublin Journal*, No. 6609.

[30] "Dictionary of National Biography," vol. li., p. 43: Ferrar's "View of Dublin," p. 76; Lewis' "Dublin Cuide:" "Sham Squire" and "Ireland before the Union;" *Dublin Journal*, Nos. 2461, 2656.

In the latter part of the eighteenth century the neighbourhood attained its zenith as a fashionable resort. Each summer the Irish Court migrated thither from Dublin Castle, and the Viceroy of the day took up his abode in the residence known as Blackrock House. This great mansion, with its noble sea front and suite of magnificent reception rooms, "with just agreement framed in every part," was erected by Mr. John Lees, then Secretary of the Irish Post Office, and afterwards created a baronet[31]. His idea in building it was, possibly, a speculative one, and it proved a very remunerative investment. To its occupation in 1778 by some distinguished person reference is doubtless made in an ironical announcement that "the poor of Blackrock were hopeful of obtaining garden produce at moderate terms on a great personage accepting a house near the town." At its landing-place the Earl of Northington, on his arrival in June, 1783, as Lord Lieutenant, stepped ashore, and there he dined before proceeding to Dublin. In its large rooms his successor, the Duke of Rutland, in July, 1785, received and entertained at breakfast an aeronaut, called Crosbie, who had made an ascent from the Duke of Leinster's lawn in Dublin the previous day, and had been rescued out at sea, where his balloon had descended. There Rutland's Secretary, Thomas Orde, afterwards Baron Bolton in the spring of 1786, recruited his health, and there, in July, 1788, Lord Charles FitzGerald, a most popular nobleman, met with a severe accident while landing from his barge. From there the Marquis of Buckingham made sea excursions to Dalkey Island and every part of the bay, and there stayed his successors, the Earls of Westmoreland and Camden; the famous Lord Castlereagh, attended by his secretaries, Cooke and Elliott; and the great Earl of Clare, Lord Chancellor of Ireland, for whose protection at the time of the Rebellion a detachment of the King's County Militia was stationed at Blackrock[32].

---

[31] The following inscription appears on a mural tablet in Monkstown Church "Sacred to the memory of the late Sir John Lees, Baronet; what he was as a husband and father, and as a Christian, is deeply engraved on the memory of his surviving family and friends and his great public and private character will remain long after this frail monument, shall perish and be forgotten—a memorial which is rather intended as a grateful and dutiful offering of the filial affection and piety of six afflicted sons than to be the record of his virtues to posterity; he died universally lamented by all ranks and descriptions of people the 3rd September, A.D. 1811, aged 74 years."

[32] "On the Rock near Dublin," a poem inscribed to John Lees, in *Hibernian Magazine* for 1800, p. 182; *Freeman's Journal*, No. 1930; *Dublin Journal*, No. 6645; *Exshaw's*

About the same time as Blackrock House, Maretimo, which also still adorns the neighbourhood, was built. It was erected by Sir Nicholas Lawless, Bart., M.P. for Lifford, who was afterwards created Baron Cloncurry, and has since remained in the possession of the successive holders of that title. Lawless was the leading merchant of his day, and attained to some distinction as a member of the House of Commons. In spite of an unattractive presence and faults of delivery, he was not unsuccessful as a speaker, and displayed in committee a knowledge of the principles of commerce and of political economy. His elevation to his baronetcy and peerage was due to unswerving support of the Government[33].

A diarist of the period gives an interesting account of an entertainment at Maretimo, at which he was present, in the first Lord Cloncurry's time. It lasted for the round of the clock, and truly was deserving of the name of a rout. It was summer, and tables were spread in large tents on the lawn, and in the open air. The company was great, and many who were unable to find room at the tables outside were reduced to dining in the house. The grounds of Blackrock House were thrown open, and after dinner the guests strolled about until dancing began, to the music of the band of the Kildare Militia. A year later a similar entertainment, only more splendid, was given by the Earl of Clonmell at Neptune. The diarist describes the numerous assemblage sitting down to luncheon, after which, the day being showery, the guests sought amusement in crowding the rooms and listening to dance music, to which their host's entreaties could not induce them to respond. At 5 o'clock the Lord Lieutenant joined the party and dinner began. It could not be served in the open air, as had been intended, on account of the rain, and "the squeeze was immense." Some of the tables had to be laid in the bedrooms and others in the hall. After dinner, which was most sumptuous, dancing began and lasted till midnight[34].

Another resident at Newtown at the same time as the first Lord Cloncurry was Mr. Robert Jephson, a dramatist and poet of some note, and

---

Magazine for 1785, p. 390; *Dublin Chronicle,* 1788-1789, pp. 56, 248, 327, 455, 519, 607- 1789-790, pp. 112, 200, 252 ; Musgrave's "Memoirs of the Irish Rebellion," vol. i., p. 228.

[33] "Falkland's Review of the Irish House of Commons," p. 75; Lease in Registry of Deeds Office.

[34] MS. Diary of Alexander Hamilton, K.C. LL.D.

a member of the Irish Parliament. He had come to Ireland with Lord Halifax, on his appointment as Lord Lieutenant. It is said that Lord Halifax was requested by Garrick, with kindly intention, to take the play-going youth to Ireland or anywhere else out of his way, as he left him no peace behind the scenes[35]. Prospect, now St. Joseph's College, was then a boarding school, where the sons of many of the nobility and gentry of Ireland were educated. It was first kept by the Rev. John Burrowes, and afterwards by the Rev. Charles Meares. Amongst Burrowes' pupils was the second Lord Cloncurry, who says that Burrowes had good qualities, but had mistaken his vocation[36].

A boarding-house with a spacious ballroom was erected at Seapoint by a Mr. William Jones towards the close of the eighteenth century. It stood near the edge of the sea, close to a well known as Tobernea, and its site is now occupied by the terrace called by that name. During the summer subscription dances were held in the ballroom, and our diarist, on going down in July, 1800, found a full room, a good set, and a tolerable supper, but execrable wine. At the time of his rebellion some of Robert Emmet's friends were staying there, and Emmet is said to have been a visitor at the house. It was subsequently proposed to purchase the house as a recruiting depôt for the army, but the negotiations fell through, and Beggars' Bush Barracks were built instead[37]. The strand at Seapoint continued to be a favourite bathing-place, and while bathing there in September, 1797, two young women were carried out of their depth. One of them was drowned; the other was rescued, but on learning the fate of her companion she became unconscious, and died in a few hours[38].

The neighbourhood of Seapoint was, in November, 1807, the scene of perhaps the greatest tragedy that ever took place in or near Dublin. On a dark winter's day two vessels, *The Princess of Wales* and *The Rochdale*, set sail from

---

[35] "Dictionary of National Biography," xxix., p. 334; "Falkland's Review of the Irish House of Commons," p. 107; O'Keeffe's "Recollections of his Life," vol. i., p. 83.

[36] Personal Recollections of Lord Cloncurry, p. 7; Fitzpatrick's "Life of Lord Cloncurry," vol. i., p. 54; *Dublin Chronicle*, 1791-1792, p. 897.

[37] Military Papers preserved in Public Record Office; Madden's "United Irishmen," 2nd ed., Ser. iii., pp. 430, 433.

[38] *Hibernian Magazine* for 1797, pt. ii., p. 280.

the mouth of the Liffey, laden with nearly 500 soldiers and officers belonging to various regiments. In the night a storm arose, and the next morning the two vessels were discovered complete wrecks on the rocks near Blackrock House. Every person on board had perished, with the exception of the captain and some of the crew of *The Princess of Wales,* who had escaped in the only boat, leaving the passengers to their fate. The shore long presented a sight too horrible for description[39].

The principal residents during the first half of the last century were the second Lord Cloncurry and the Rev. Sir Harcourt Lees, Bart., men who, in their political opinions, exhibited the opposite extremes. The former, who resided constantly at Maretimo, was a man of the most liberal views, who had been suspected in early life of revolutionary sentiments. The latter, who dwelt in his father's home, the gates of which he had sheeted with iron, was a man of the strictest type of Conservatism, and has been described "as the renowned, the dreaded, and the dreadless Sir Harcourt"[40].

BLACKROCK.

THE town of Blackrock lies at the extremity of the franchises of the city of Dublin, and the cross, which stands in its main street, marks the termination of the ancient jurisdiction of the Dublin Corporation. The cross is generally thought to have been erected for that purpose, but it has recently been suggested that it is ecclesiastical in its origin. The place is one of the points mentioned in the accounts of the riding of the franchises, but, except in connection with that event, was little known until the middle of the eighteenth century. It then became, under the name of the Black Rock, the holiday outlet for the Dublin populace. Thither they proceeded in crowds on Sundays and high days on the cars of the period. These cars have been described by a contemporary writer as the drollest and most diverting conveyances imaginable, and were primitive in their construction. Two long shafts, a few boards, and a pair of very low wheels, cut out of a solid block,

---

[39] *Cyclopædian Magazine* for 1807, p. 703-1808, p. 64.
[40] "Dictionary of National Biography," vol. xxxii., pp. 245, 394; *Dublin and London Magazine* for 1825, pp. 237, 308.

made the vehicle, on which a feather bed was laid, and six persons sat with their feet hanging down, almost touching the ground.

For the accommodation of the people houses of entertainment, which are marked on the view of the coast taken at that time, were opened, and Blackrock became celebrated for its immense consumption of claret and spirituous liquors. The principal inn in 1764 was "The Sign of the Ship," to which a spacious ballroom was attached, and where an excellent band of music, a man cook, and a good larder were to be found, and, twenty years later, "The Three Tun Tavern," which was kept by one Bishop, a worthy host was renowned for its good cheer. The narrowness of the approaches to the town and the precipitous slopes to the sea were the source of frequent accidents. Bathing fatalities were also not uncommon, and with the hope of lessening them, there was, in 1754, a proposal to build a bathing place. Blackrock was the scene, in 1754, of the suicide of Sir Charles Moore, which caused much excitement at the time, and, in 1768, of an attempt by a servant to poison an entire family; also, in 1775, it was selected as the place for a duel which, on one of the combatants, "in a gentlemanlike manner," firing in the air, was happily compromised. While the Lords Lieutenants were resident at Blackrock House, we read that the Rock experienced "the sweets of dissipation to so high a degree that even Bath could scarce take the lead for more gaiety, amusement, and *bon ton*," and fruit shows, known as Melon Feasts, were then instituted, at which the gardeners of the Lord Lieutenant, the Archbishop of Dublin, and other notabilities bore away elegant gold medals[41].

---

[41] "The Cross of Blackrock," by Patrick J. O'Reilly, in *Journal, R.S.A.I.*, vol. xxxi., p. 385 *Pue's Occurrences*, vol. xxxii., No. 64, vol. No. 70. vol. lvii., No. 60, vol. lxi., No. 6297, vol. lxv., No. 6758 ; *Dublin Journal*, No. 6860 ; *Freeman's Journal*, vol. v., No. 6, vol. xii., No. 92 ; *Dublin Chronicle.* 1788-1789. p. 367 ; *Hibernian Magazine*, 1794, pt. ii., p. 286-1801, p. 514 ; "Hibernia Curiosa," pp. 15, 25; "Historical Manuscripts Commission," Rept. xii., pt. x., p. 198; Blacker's "Sketches of Booterstown," pp. 74, 774.

Montpelier Parade in 1802.
From a Plate "The Hibernian Magazine"

MONTPELIER AND ITS NEIGHBOURHOOD.

THE name Montpelier is now mainly preserved by a row of houses called Montpelier Parade, on the road from Blackrock to Monkstown. These houses date from about the time of the Union, when they were erected by Mr. Molesworth Green, but the name Montpelier had been applied previously to a dwelling near their site. In 1748 an auction of furniture, which included a telescope of the newest and best kind, was advertised to be held for Mr. Thomas Byrne, at Montpelier, near Newtown Castle Byrne, and a house there on which he had laid out £2.500, was afterwards advertised to be sold[42]. This house appears in the picture at the end of the parade, and is now called Shandon.

Entrance to Rockfield.
From a photography by Thomas Mason

---

[42] *Dublin Journal*, No.2197; *Pue's Occurrences*, vol. lviii., No. 21.

Rockfield
From a Photography by Thomas Mason

The great residence in the neighbourhood in the eighteenth century was Rockfield, in Newtown-Park-avenue. Its ground were then much more extensive than at present, and stretched down to Blackrock, where the places called Dunardagh and Craigmore now stand. The house, though it has been enlarged and altered, still retains much of its original plan, and, from the style of architecture exhibited in its construction, has been thought to be of French design. It was selected by Lord Townshend, towards the close of his viceroyalty, which terminated in 1772, as his summer retreat, and probably it was under his direction, in memory of his military exploits with Wolfe, before Quebec, that the martial emblems, with the words "Britain's Glory" underneath, which adorn the staircase, were executed. There Townshend could indulge undisturbed in the scenes of revelry and dissipation in which he delighted, and there, in company with Provost Andrews and Attorney-General Tisdal, then his neighbour at Stillorgan, he doubtless often proved himself deserving of his character as an eight-bottle man. One of his last acts before leaving Ireland was to send £40 to the curate of Monkstown for distribution amongst the poor—a gift, let us hope, actuated as much by charity as by the desire for popularity, which was so strong a trait of his character[43]. Rockfield was afterwards assigned by its owner, Mr. Thomas Manning, to Sir Frederick Flood, Bart, King's Counsel, and M.P. for Wexford, a most popular politician, and one of the strongest opponents of the Union. It was subsequently sold to Mr. Edward Badham Thornhill, and was afterwards occupied by the celebrated Sir Boyle Roche, whose admirable discharge of his duties as Gentleman Usher and Master of the Ceremonies in Dublin Castle, has been lost sight of amidst the innumerable anecdotes of his bull-making propensities[44].

There were several other residences at that time in the neighbourhood occupied by persons of position. William Raphson, whose three nieces married respectively Bishop Stock, of Killala; Bishop Newcome, of Waterford, afterwards Primate; and Archdeacon Palmer, and whose name is honoured as a benefactor of the Rotunda Hospital, lived for many years near Newtown Park[45]; as did, also, the second Earl of Mayo, who died near Blackrock, in 1792[46]; Christopher Myers, the architect of the Chapel of Trinity College, and father of a distinguished officer and baronet, who died at Myersville, now Wynberg, in 1789[47], and Joseph Atkinson, a well-known *litterateur* and Deputy-Judge Advocate-General, who died in 1818, at Melfield[48].

Later on we find among the residents Sir Edward Newenham, who died at Ratino in 1814, a politician whose services in Parliament earned him the name of a patriot, and Sir William Betham, who died at Montpelier in 1853, for

---

[43] *Freeman's Journal*, No. 1117 vol. xv., No. 18.

[44] "Dictionary of National Biography," vol. xix., p. 330, vol. xlix., p. 66; "Studies in Irish History and Biography," by C. Litton Falkiner, p. 228 ; Leases in Registry of Deeds Office ; *Dublin Evening Post*, Feb. 6, 1794.

[45] *Dublin Journal*, No. 6885; *Dublin Chronicle*, 1789-1790, p. 168; *Dublin Evening Mail*, Oct. 21, 1899; "History of the Lying-in Hospital," by Edward Evans, in *The Irish Builder* for 1897, p. 57.

[46] *Exshaw's Magazine* for 1792, p. 222; "Post Chaise Companion," ed. 1786.

[47] *Exshaw's Magazine* for 1789, p. 392; Ferrar's "View of Dublin," p. 17; Burke's "Extinct Baronetcy."

[48] "Dictionary of National Biography," vol. ii., p. 224; *Cyclopædian Magazine* for 1808, p. 481; Ferrar's "View of Dublin," p. 77.

many years Ulster King of Arms, whose birthplace, Stradbrook, in Surrey, probably gave its name to the adjoining village[49].

THE PORT OF KINGSTOWN.

(Formerly known as the Port of Dunleary.)

WITHIN Kingstown Harbour, at its south-west corner, there is a small pier used by colliers. This pier formerly enclosed the harbour of Dunleary, and, up to the time of the construction of the refuge harbour of Kingstown, was the only shelter for vessels on the coast between Wexford and Dublin. Dunleary, a name which is supposed to be derived from the place having been the site of a dun, or fort, erected in the fifth century by Leaghaire, King of Ireland, first came into notice in the time of the Commonwealth as a landing-place for the ships of war, which lay out in the bay. A fishery, which probably had been established in the time of the Monks of St. Mary's Abbey, existed there, and Ludlow mentions that, when leaving Ireland in 1655, he gained the ship in which he was to cross the Channel by means of one of the largest of the herring vessels which lay in the creek below Monkstown. From that time, although Ringsend was the usual place of embarkation and disembarkation, the creek of Dunleary, which is now crossed by the railway, was occasionally made use of by travellers to or from England, and a quay was built. In the Restoration period the Earl of Essex, on his arrival as Lord Lieutenant, landed there, and the appointment of an excise officer indicates the increasing importance of the port, which became the constant station of a man-of-war[50].

A poet of the period commemorates the departure from Dunleary, in September, 1709, of their Excellencies the Earl and Countess of Wharton. He describes seeing, from Killiney's craggy height, two warlike vessels, gay with bunting, prepared to carry away the ruler of the land, and how the people gave way to grief and sighs, which he calls on them to suppress, since the destiny of

---

[49] "Dictionary of National Biography," vol. iv., p. 424, vol. xl., p. 333 "Falkland's Review of the Irish House of Commons," p. 93.

[50] *Joyce's* "Irish Names of Places," ed. 1895, vol. i., p. 140; "Memoirs of Edmund Ludlow," ed. by C. H. Firth, vol. i., p. 425; "Liber Munerum"; King's "State of the Protestants of Ireland," p. 323; Monkstown Parish Register.

their happy isle is committed to such Lords Justices as the famed Cæsar, General Ingoldsby, and the learned Lycurgus, Lord Chancellor Freeman, who, "like comely twins, combined to fight its battles and protect its laws." Swift, who sailed in the Government yacht in the following year, gives the Dunleary boatmen a bad character, and relates how they made him double their remuneration under threat of losing the yacht, for which he found he was in ample time. In 1741, James O'Hara, second Lord Tyrawley, then Ambassador to Portugal, landed at Dunleary, from His Majesty's ship *Lymm*, which he had joined at Cork, where he had arrived in the Lisbon packet-boat; and, in 1743, Richard Annesley, sixth Earl of Anglesey, landed there, and proceeded to his seat at Bray, on his arrival to defend his title against the claimant, James Annesley. Early in the morning of a September day, in 1753, their Excellencies the Duke and Duchess of Dorset arrived in the bay in *The Dorset* yacht, and were put on shore at Dunleary by their barge about 8 o'clock. They had been expected to land at Ringsend, where great preparations had been made to receive them with concerts of music, guns, and pedereroes. Most of the performers were unable to reach Dunleary in time, but many persons of importance went out in boats to pay their compliments to their Excellencies before they disembarked. On shore their Excellencies were awaited by the coaches and servants of the Lords Justices, and proceeded to town amongst crowds, who expressed their joy by loud acclamations. The journals of the day specially note the selection by the Duchess of Irish poplin for the material of her dress[51].

Though less fashionable than Newtown Castle Byrne, Dunleary was then a seaside place of amusement. Swift, writing in 1721 to his sub-Dean, asks him how often he had been with his wife to Dunleary, and about the same time some verses appeared, which invited the ladies of Dublin to repair in coach or on car to Dunleary, where they would find honest residents and could procure good ale. Such luxuries as meat and wine they were recommended to bring with them. Dunleary was also possessed of at least one good dwelling, known as the Great House. In it probably died, in 1711, Lady Mary Sheares, of Dunleary, daughter of Richard, second Earl of Barrymore, and wife, first of the

---

[51] "The Diverting Post," preserved in Trinity College Library; Scott's "Works of Swift," vol. ii., p. 7; *Pue's Occurrences,* vol. xxxvii., No. 57, vol. xl., No. 71; "Dictionary of National Biography," vol. ii., p. 62; vol. xlii., p. 62; *Dublin Journal,* Nos. 2757, 2758.

Rev. Gerald Barry, and secondly, of the Rev. Christopher Sheares, of Tandragee, and in it resided, successively, Lord Tullamore, afterwards Earl of Charleville; Lord Southwell, and Viscount Lanesborough. Later on Mr. John Carden, ancestor of the Cardens of Fishmoyne, leased a large place near Dunleary, which comprised lands known as the Seafield, the Rockfield, and the Towerfield, and which was bounded on one side by the sea, and on the other by the high road from Monkstown to Bullock. A fishery still existed—in 1751 the Dunleary fishermen brought to shore a shark, the first ever caught there—but from the hopes expressed that foreign fishermen might be induced to settle near Dublin, and that the city might be then supplied with fresh fish, it cannot have been carried on with much vigour. The inhabitants of the village were, owing to the frequent presence of men-of-war in the bay, constantly liable to be pressed for service in the navy, and, in 1757, during an attempt of the kind, shots were fired, and one of the townsmen was wounded[52].

Dunleary Pier in 1795.
From a Plate Drawn by F. Jukes

---

[52] Scott's "Works of Swift," vol. xvi., p. 375; "A Petition to the Ladies of Dublin from Dunleary," preserved in Trinity College Library; Monkstown Parish Register; Prerogative Grant of Tutelage to Lady Sheares; Burke's "Extinct Peerage,"; *Dublin Journal,* No. 1885; Lease in Registry of Heeds Office; Steele's "Events in Ireland." preserved in Bodleian Library, Oxford; *Dublin Journal,* No. 2592 *Pue's Occurrences,* vol. liv., No. 59.

The necessity for building a pier at Dunleary was in 1755, represented to the Irish House of Commons, in a petition signed by inhabitants of Dublin. The petition set forth the danger which often attended the navigation of the Dublin port, and the advantages which Dunleary presented as a site for a harbour. The House granted the prayer of the petition, and voted a sum of £21.000 for the erection of the pier. Its erection occupied twelve years, the actual sum expended being only £18,500. Its completion was superintended by the well-known archæologist, General Vallancey. Before it was actually finished it proved of service. In the summer of 1764, two men-of-war, *The Wasp* and *The Ranger*, were repaired alongside, and during storms in the winter of that year seven or eight vessels were safely harboured under its shelter. It was then hoped that when the old quay was taken down, and some rocks at the end of the bay removed, there would be room for twenty sail at a time to anchor under its protection. This anticipation was, however, unduly optimistic. The harbour looked well. Austin Cooper, who probably saw it when the tide was full, describes it as a handsome, semi-circular harbour, enclosed by high banks of gravel, and by the pier, which was about 27 perches long, and which sheltered it from all winds except the north. But for practical purposes it proved, like many of the small harbours since constructed a complete failure. It soon filled up with sand, which the dredging machines of the time were unable to remove; and in 1776, a correspondent, styling himself "Hawser Trunnion," drew attention to its inutility, and expressed the opinion that the pier had been built in the wrong direction. The condition of the harbour was brought under the notice of the House of Commons, by a petition signed, amongst others, by Lord Chancellor Hewitt, who was then living at Stillorgan, and by Viscount Ranelagh; and a Committee, presided over by Sir Nicholas Lawless, recommended the expenditure of an additional sum of £1,150 upon the pier[53].

The Viceroys and their families continued to make use occasionally of Dunleary on their arrival or departure. There the Duke of Bedford, in 1758, embarked on *The Dorset* yacht, which was conveyed to England by *The Biddefort*, of twenty tons, and there again, two years later, having been accompanied from town by the nobility and gentry in their coaches and six,

---

[53] Journals of the Irish House of Commons; *Dublin Journal*, No. 3919; Cooper's Note Book; *Exshaw's Magazine* for 1776, p. 101.

he embarked on the same boat, under convoy of *The Surprise*. There landed, in 1780, the Earl of Carlisle, who had crossed from Parkgate, on the Dee, in *The Dorset* yacht, which was commanded by Sir Alexander Schomberg, and convoyed by *The Stag*, frigate, and *The Townshend*, revenue cruiser; in 1784 the Duchess of Rutland and her three children; in 1787 the Marquis of Buckingham, who proceeded to Mr. Lees' villa; in 1789, the Marchioness of Buckingham, who also went to "The Rock," and, in 1790, the Countess of Westmoreland[54].

The Coffee House at Dunleary in 1803.
From Plate in "The Hibernian Magazine."

The packets from England then went to Ringsend, but passengers were sometimes put on shore, by means of boats, at Dunleary, when the wind was contrary. For their accommodation a coffee-house, remains of which still exist, was opened near the pier. Possibly it was the same house as the one known by the sign of the "Star and Garter," which was, in 1754, advertised to be sold—a house described as fit for any nobleman or gentleman. Dunleary was at that time an inconsiderable and dirty village, the abode of a few fishermen; and the country between it and Bullock was a sterile tract, covered

---

[54] *Exshaw's Magazine* for 1758, p. 311, 1760, p. 290, 1781, p. 58, 1784, p. 223; *Dublin Chronicle*, 1787-1788, p. 799, 1789-1790, p. 992 *Hibernian Magazine* for 1789, p. 333.

with furze and heath, and traversed by a few footpaths. The principal resident near the village was Mr. William Roseingrave, one of the Secretaries in Dublin Castle, whose house stood on or near the site of Salthill Hotel. He had filled several offices, and belonged to a family renowned for their musical talents. His father had been organist of the Dublin Cathedrals, and his uncle, who died in his house at Salthill, in 1766, was a talented, though eccentric, composer. The house and lands of Dunleary belonged then to Sir James Taylor, Lord Mayor of Dublin in 1765; and another resident of note was the revenue surveyor, Mr. George Glover, who gave elegant entertainments on *The Newtown* barge, and was presented with the thanks of the Corporation of Weavers for his exertions to prevent the smuggling of foreign silks. A humble resident, of the name of Lawlor also deserves record, on account of the extraordinary feat, which he frequently performed, about 1760, of swimming from Dunleary to Howth; and an African diver ought not to be forgotten, who in 1783 attracted crowds to Dunleary to see his descents under the sea in a diving bell[55].

Projects in connection with the Mail Packet service from England, which would have affected Dunleary, had been more than once mooted. In 1778 it was announced that a new pier was to be built there, from which all packets were to sail. In 1790 much conjecture was aroused in the neighbourhood by the packets anchoring in the man-of-war roads, where the mails were put on board by wherries, and, in 1801, there was a scheme to make a deep sea harbour at Dalkey, and to connect Dalkey with Dublin by means of a canal. But it was not until 1809 that the proposal to construct the present harbour at Kingstown was made. In that year a petition was presented to the Lord Lieutenant, praying that the construction of an asylum harbour near Dunleary should be undertaken by the Government, and, six years later, an Act was passed, authorising the work, at an estimated cost of £505,000. The first stone of the East Pier was laid, in 1817, by His Excellency the Earl of Whitworth, and the embarkation from the head of that pier of His Majesty George IV., after his visit to Ireland in 1821, gave origin to the familiar name

---

[55] *Universal Advertiser*, No. 124 "Dictionary of National Biography," vol. xlix, p. 245; *Dublin Journal*, No. 4087; "History of St. Audoen's Church," in *The Irish Builder* for 1887, p. 192; *Pue's Occurrences*, vol. lxviii., No. 7007; *Dublin Journal*, No.3672, 3962; O'Keeffe's "Recollections of his Life," vol. i., p. 385; *Dublin Journal*, No. 6667.

of Kingstown Harbour. Even at that early stage of its construction its future utility was foreshadowed. It was on Monday, September 3, late in the afternoon, that the King embarked on his yacht, but, owing to high winds, it was not until the following Friday that he could set out for England. On Wednesday his yacht hoisted sail, and put out along the coast of Wicklow, but she was soon driven back, and was glad to remain under the shelter of the pier until the storm abated. The stone of which the piers are built, was quarried out of Dalkey Hill, and was brought to Dunleary in trucks, drawn by horses on four railroads, laid side by side. So fast was the granite poured into the sea that the East Pier is said to have progressed at the rate of 100 feet a month[56].

BULLOCK.

THE Castle of Bullock, to which a modern house has been attached, forms a conspicuous object on the road from Kingstown to Dalkey. It stands between the road and the sea, and overhangs a creek, now converted into a harbour. Mr. J. H. Parker, C.B., an eminent authority on Gothic architecture, who inspected the Castle in 1859, formed the opinion that it was a structure of the twelfth century. He says that it is built of plain and rude masonry, and that in plan it is a simple oblong. The lower story is vaulted throughout, and the rooms in it, he thought, were probably used as a store-house. Above the vault the Castle is divided into two unequal portions. In the larger division there are two principal rooms, one over the other, with small, round-headed windows and doorways; each of these rooms is provided with a fireplace, and there is a garderobe in a turret at one corner, and a small closet in another, with a staircase between. The smaller division of the house is divided into three stories, above the vaults, probably for bedrooms; there are no fireplaces, and the windows are square-headed. The two ends of the building are higher than the centre, but, in Mr. Parker's opinion, it is all part of one design and was built together; the battlements are in the form of steps. Under one portion of the Castle there is an archway, probably used to pass from one courtyard to

---

[56] *Hibernian Magazine* for 1778, p. 247, 1801, p. 514; *Dublin Chronicle*, 1790-1791, p. 296; Warburton, Whitelaw, and Walsh's "History of Dublin," vol. i., p. 1273; *Saunder's News Letter*, Sept. 4-8, 1821.

another, and there were, when Parker made his inspection, remains of a bawn, as well as of a tower, which has since disappeared, but which stood about 100 yards from the Castle on the Dalkey side[57].

Bullock Castle.
From a Drawing by W. F. Wakeman.

Bullock was, doubtless, known in times long prior to the English settlement as the site of a rocking-stone, which stood on its lands near the Castle, until the destructive hand of man removed it, at the beginning of the nineteenth century. The Castle, as we have seen, in the history of the coeval edifice at Monkstown, was built by the Cistercian Monks of the Abbey of the Blessed Virgin Mary, near Dublin, and was erected by them to protect the fishery, which rose to such great proportions, under their auspices, on the portion of the lands of Carrickbrennan known as Bullock. In return for the encouragement and protection which they gave to the fishermen, the monks

---

[57] "Observations on the Ancient Domestic Architecture of Ireland," in *Archæologia*, vol. xxxviii., p. 163.

exacted a toll of fish from every vessel using the port, and, in the fourteenth century, this custom gave rise to litigation between the Abbey and the fishermen, in which the Abbey was successful. The land immediately round the Castle, as in the case of Monkstown, was retained by the monks in their own hands, and, in 1312, the enemies of the King carried off from the grange of Bullock corn and other property belonging to the Abbey. There was frequent opportunity at Bullock for the extension of the hospitality for which the Order was famous, and many a traveller, doubtless, found a resting-place within the Castle. There, probably, the boy Lord Lieutenant, Prince Thomas of Lancaster, son of Henry IV., on his arrival from England, in the chilly month of November in the year 1401, partook of refreshments, and there Henry VIII.'s Solicitor-General for Ireland, Walter Cowley, spent a night on his arrival from London, in March, 1539, with money of the State in his charge[58].

Rocking Stone at Bullock in 1777.
From a Drawing by Gabriel Beranger.

At the time of the dissolution of St. Mary's Abbey there were on the lands of Bullock, a portion of which was covered with firs and underwood, besides the Castle, two houses and six cottages. The town appears to have been strongly

---

[58] "Chartularies of St. Mary's Abbey," vol. i., pp. xl., xlii.; Patent and Close Rolls, p. 160; "Dictionary of National Biography," vol. lvi., p. 158; "Communication between London and Dublin," in *The Irish Builder* for 1897, p. 35.

guarded with walls, into which at least one tower was built, and to have contained a church. Two tenants, Patrick Berminghain and John Gaban, were in occupation, and the tithes, which were payable in fish, were leased to Richard Edwards. After the suppression of the Abbey, the Castle and its lands were leased by the Crown in 1542, in consideration of the surrender of Powerscourt, and other neighbouring lands, to Peter Talbot, of Fassaroe, near Bray. Thirteen years later, on St. Andrew's Day, 1555, Talbot met a violent death, possibly while protecting his property from a party of kerns, such as we find some years later waging war at Bullock against the militia; and his son being then only an infant, his possessions were for a time in the custody of his son's guardian, Christopher, twentieth Baron of Howth, known as the Blind Lord[59].

At the beginning of the seventeenth century the town contained as many as thirty houses. The Castle was in good repair, but the tower was ruinous. The port continued to be used occasionally by other vessels besides fishing craft. In 1559, the Earl of Sussex, then Lord Deputy, landed there, and, in 1633, a Dutch ship, while lying under the walls of the Castle, was taken by a privateer, called *The True Love,* commanded by Captain Thomas Gayner, who claimed to have letters of marque from the King of Spain—an occurrence which gave rise to international difficulty. During the sixteenth century the Castle and the lands had been assigned by the Talbots to members of one of the great Dublin mercantile families of the day, the Fagans, whose principal residence was Feltrim, near Swords, and whose ancestors had been amongst the earliest English settlers; and we find amongst the members of the family in possession of Bullock, Christopher Fagan and his younger brother, Richard, each of whom filled the high position of Mayor of Dublin[60].

When the great Rebellion broke out in October, 1641, the eldest son of Richard Fagan, Mr. John Fagan, was in occupation of the Castle, and, whether from compulsion or inclination, appears, from depositions afterwards made, to have rendered the rebels much assistance. One of the first efforts to reduce to

---

[59] "Chartularies of St. Mary's Abbey," vol. ii., p. 64; Fiants, Henry viii. No, 283; Elizabeth, Nos. 1158, 1779; Exchequer Inquisition, Philip and Mary, No. 8.

[60] "Liber Munerum"; "Calendar of Domestic State Papers," 1633; Knowler's "Life of Strafford," vol. i., p. 131 "Calendar of Patent Rolls, James I," p. 43; "Pedigree of the Fagans of Feltrim," by G. D. Burtchaell, in *The Irish Builder* for 1887, p. 85, and 1888, p. 78; Patent and Close Rolls, p. 43; Chancery Inquisitions, Jac. I., No. 19.

obedience the neighbourhood of Dublin was made at Bullock, and it was the scene of cruel retaliation for the outrages which had been committed. A month after the rising a party of soldiers, under the command of Colonel Lawrence Crawford, an officer of more courage than judgment, descended on the village, and, finding that the inhabitants on their approach had put to sea, the soldiers pursued them in boats, and threw them—men, women and children, to the number of fifty-six—overboard. All through that winter the southern part of the County Dublin remained at the mercy of the rebels. Shortly before Christmas, John Fagan came from Feltrim to his Castle at Bullock and, according to the evidence of his servant, finding no provisions ready for him, went on to Carrickmines Castle, which belonged to his relatives, the Walshes. It was the headquarters of the rebels, and to it he sent, subsequently, from Bullock supplies of fish and a small cannon, which had been on the battlements. In the following March Carrickmines Castle was levelled with the ground, and, a few weeks later, another descent was made on Bullock, this time by Colonel Gibson's regiment, and some of the men found there were killed and others brought prisoners to Dublin. The Castle was then seized by the Crown, and a garrison of soldiers was maintained in it until the Commonwealth was established in Ireland. At first the garrison was in charge of Colonel Crawford, but, on the cessation with the Irish, he joined the army of the Parliament in England, and a Captain Richard Newcomen succeeded him. In Newcomen's time the garrison consisted of seven non-commissioned officers and sixty men, under command of himself, Lieutenant Valentine Wood, and Ensign Arthur Whitehead, the weekly charge for the soldiers being £7, and for the officers £1 3s. In 1644 the defences of the Castle were strengthened by the construction of a rampart, furnished with three cannon, which were conveyed to Bullock by boat under a military escort, and the erection of a guard house. The estimated cost of this work, which appears to have been exceeded, was £25; brick was the material used, and masons, carpenters, carters, and labourers, who were fed from the regimental canteen, were employed[61].

---

[61] Clarendon's "History of the Rebellion and Civil War in Ireland," Lon. 1721, p. 341; "Dictionary of National Biography," vol. xiii, p. 52; Depositions of 1641; "A True Relation of the Chief Passages in Ireland," Lon. 1642, preserved in the National Library of Ireland; Historical Manuscripts Commission, Rept. viii. App. p. 594; Rept. xiv., App., pt. vii., p. 180; Ormonde Papers, preserved in Kilkenny Castle.

At the time of the Battle of Rathmines the authorities of the Parliament had friends at Bullock, and the garrison had probably joined their forces. During the Commonwealth Bullock, owing to the anchorage of the warships near it, was like Dunleary, a place of importance, and soldiers, doubtless, were kept in the Castle. In 1656 Captain Richard Roe, who was buried at Lusk, died there, and, in 1659, Captain Abraham Aldgate, who was reprimanded for giving assistance to Edmund Ludlow, and who pleaded lack of intelligence to understand the marvellous changes of the time, fled thither on horseback from Dublin, and took refuge on his ship. The inhabitants were not left without religious consolation and, in 1658, the Rev. Nathaniel Hoyle, B.D., a Fellow of Trinity College, and afterwards a prebendary in Emly Diocese, was paid £100 a year by the Parliament for acting as minister of Bullock[62].

At the time of the Restoration Bullock was stated to be "a fair ancient town of fishing"; its slated Castle and bawn were in good repair, the haven was accounted a safe one, and there was a population of fifteen English and ninety-five Irish, inhabiting some twenty houses. John Fagan had died shortly after the Rebellion, in 1643, and had been succeeded by his grandson, Christopher Fagan. The latter had been of service to the Royalist Army in the later years of Charles the First's reign, and, on the Restoration, was restored as an innocent Roman Catholic to all the family possessions, including the Castle and lands of Bullock, and the revenue from chief fish, tithe fish, customs, and fish and corn tithe. The Fagan family, however, did not long remain in possession, as Richard Fagan, who succeeded his father, Christopher Fagan, on his death, in 1683, was, after the Revolution, attainted for treason committed at Swords, and his property all confiscated. Bullock and its lands were sold by the Crown, and purchased, for £1,750, by Colonel Allen, of Stillorgan, afterwards the first Viscount Allen, whose representative, the Earl of Carysfort, is now the owner of the soil. The Rectory and tithes were at the same time given to augment the vicarages of

---

[62] Macray's "Calendar of the Clarendon Papers," vol. ii., p. 16; D'Alton's "History of the County Dublin," p. 415; "Calendar of Domestic State Papers," 1659-1660; Commonwealth Papers in Public Record Office.

Kill-of-the-Grange and Stillorgan, then under the charge of the curate of Monkstown, and possessing no church of their own[63].

So far back as the time of Charles I. there had been a revenue officer at Bullock, and, after the Restoration, one Jenkin Hopkins applied for that position. In the beginning of the eighteenth century the office was no sinecure and, in addition to his duties with regard to the revenue, the officer had to watch the illegal exportation of recruits for the French service. A detachment of soldiers was, in 1731, sent to Bullock, to prevent the embarkation of men thus enlisted, and only arrived in time to find that "the wild geese," to the number of forty, had flown the preceding night, in company with some French officers. The prevention of smuggling led often to serious rioting and, in 1735, a great battle took place at Bullock, in consequence of the seizure of a quantity of brandy and tea, and one of the revenue officers was wounded and two of the smugglers killed. In 1743 a Mr. Anthony Robinson filled the position of riding officer at Bullock, and displayed much activity in seizing whiskey concealed in churns, as well as chocolate, seal skins, and tortoise shell, which were being brought from Galway to Dublin[64].

One of the principal residents at Bullock in the Restoration period was Mr. Kenelm Livinglyhurst, who was buried, in 1685, in the Chancel of Dalkey Church, and on the purchase of Bullock, in 1703, by Colonel Allen, a Mr. Simon Young was the tenant. Subsequently the whole of the place was held under the Viscounts Allen by Mr. John Watson, a gentleman who exhibited much benevolence and humanity to his poorer neighbours, and to shipwrecked mariners, and who occupied a comfortable house, which he had built under the shelter of Bullock Castle. His son, Mr. James Watson, a popular and clever young man, was killed, in 1760, while attending horse races at Bray by a blow from the loaded handle of a whip. A writer of the period says that the house was remarkable for the beauty of its situation, especially during a storm, when the waves dashed against the rocks and fell back in cascades, sending clouds of foam over the roof, but that it was still

---

[63] Fleetwood's Survey; Down Survey Census of 1659; Carte Papers; Decrees of Innocents, iv., 42; Hearth Money Roll; Chancery Inquisition, Jas. II., No. 37; Exchequer Inquisition, Wm. and Mary, Nos. 2, 5, Wm. III., No. 1 Book of Postings and Sale.

[64] *Dublin Weekly Journal* for 1735, p. 67; "Primate Boulter's Letter," vol. ii., p. 33; *Pue's Occurrences,* vol. xl., No. 49.

more remarkable for the hospitality and politeness which reigned within, and which made it the meeting-place for all the well-bred people of the neighbourhood.

Over the rocky country by which Bullock was surrounded, foxhounds, in those days, often pursued their game, chasing Reynard through Bullock, and across the open land known as Monkstown Common, which lay between Dunleary and Monkstown into the shrubby woods for which Glenageary was famous. The ancient town of Bullock, though much decayed, still exhibited at that time a complete walled town in miniature, and contained remains of a church as well as of the tower. A quay of hewn stone had been built and, towards the close of the eighteenth century, the town contained a number of cabins occupied by fishermen, who found a ready market in Dublin for the cod, haddock, herrings, crabs, and lobsters which they caught. At the beginning of the nineteenth century, a lifeboat was placed there but, owing to the difficulty attending its launching, it was only capable of use in the finest weather. As the century went on Bullock was more and more superseded by the modern Kingstown[65].

ECCLESIASTICAL HISTORY OF MONKSTOWN.

THE Old Church, remains of which are still to be seen in the ancient graveyard of Carrickbrennan, on the opposite side of the road to the Castle of Monkstown, stood on the site of a place of worship which was dedicated to St. Mochonna, Bishop of Holm Patrick, who is supposed to have flourished about the sixth century. After the English Conquest, the latter, then known as the Chapel of Carrickbrennan was given, together with the advowson and tithes, to St. Mary s Abbey, but did not long remain in the possession of the Cistercian establishment. In 1220, Ralph de Bristol, then Treasurer of St. Patrick's Cathedral, and afterwards Bishop of Kildare, claimed portion of the tithes of Carrickbrennan, in right of the prebend of Clonkeen, or Kill-of-the-Grange—a stall which he held with the treasurership—and the Abbey, by

---

[65] Monkstown Parish Register; *Pue's Occurrences*, vol. lvii., Nos. 54,61; Wilson's "Topographical Description of Dalkey" in *Exshaw's Magazine* for 1770, p. 485; Mozeen's "Miscellaneous Essays," p. 33.

undertaking to pay him annually a certain sum, besides his costs, admitted that he had acquired a right over the spiritualities of Carrickbrennan. Subsequently the Church of Kill-of-the-Grange was exchanged by St. Patrick's Cathedral for Ballymore, the property of the Priory of the Holy Trinity and, in 1240, was confirmed to the latter religions house, which owned the land on which it stood. At the same time the Chapel of Carrickbrennan was transferred to the care of the Priory, and became attached as a chapel to the Mother Church of Kil-of-the-Grange. The great tithes were retained by St. Mary's Abbey, and the small tithes were given for the support of a chaplain. At the close of the thirteenth century the latter were insufficient for that purpose, but, doubtless, fifty years later, when one Andrew received a pair of shoes for looking after the interests of the Priory at Carrickbrennan, they had improved[66].

After the dissolution of St. Mary's Abbey, the advowson of the church and the tithes, excepting those of the lands of Bullock and Newtown, were given to Sir John Travers, and were subsequently held, in spite of their being Roman Catholics, by his successors. The advowson, however, was taken from them before 1615, when the Church was in sequestration, and the Dean of Christ Church, as successor of the Prior of the Holy Trinity, had probably, before 1630, established his right to the parish. The Rev. William Morris Lloyd was then in charge of it, as well as of the parishes of Dalkey and Killiney, as curate, and he was succeeded by the Rev. John Davis, who also held the cures of Kilmacinoge, Old Connaught, and Kilternan. In 1642 the latter had, to divide the pittance he received for Monkstown—some £6 a year—with another clergyman, the Rev. Randolph Foxwist, then curate of Leperstown, who was connected with the Cheevers family. The great tithes were still owned by Travers descendants, and were held by Sir Gerald Aylmer and Henry Cheevers. At that time there was also in Monkstown a Roman Catholic Church, which was served, in 1630, by the Rev. Turlogh O'Brien[67].

---

[66] Fiant, Elizabeth, No. 3146; O'Hanlon's "Lives of the Irish Saints," vol. i., p. 193; "Chartularies of St. Mary's Abbey," vol. i., pp. 85, 189; Christ Church Deeds Nos. 51, 150, 235.

[67] Regal Visitation of 1615; Archbishop Bulkeley's Report; Diocesan Records.

Ruined Church of Monkstown in 1835.
From a Woodcut in "The Dublin Penny Journal."

During the Commonwealth, St. Mochonna's Church, which was, in Charles the First's reign, in good repair, though "wanting in decency and some necessaries," fell into ruin, owing to disuse, and some years after the Restoration it was completely rebuilt, through the munificence of Mr. Edward Corker, who had the work executed entirely at his own expense. The building is described by Mr. Austin Cooper as being very plain and small, the only ornament being a weathercock, which bore the letters E.C., and the date, 1668, of its erection[68]. There was then no church fit for use in the parishes of Kill-of-the-Grange, Dalkey, Killiney, Tully, Stillorgan, and Kilmacud, and these parishes were united to Monkstown, and continued to be served for nearly one hundred years by the curate of Monkstown. The tithes, both great and small, were restored to the Church, and were at the disposal of the Dean of Christ Church, who, as rector, appointed the curates. The first who acted in that capacity was the Rev. Thomas Ward, afterwards Dean of Connor[69], and he was succeeded, in 1685, by the Rev. William Deane, a Welshman, and

---

[68] Cooper's Note Book.
[69] Cotton's "Fasti Ecclesiæ Hibernicæ;" Monkstown Parish Register.

a scholar of Trinity College, who also held the curacies of St. Catherine's and St. James's parishes in Dublin[70]. Then, for the long period of more than fifty years, commencing in 1690, the cure was served by the Rev. Alan Maddison, a native of the County Fermanagh, and a graduate of Dublin University. His income was augmented by his appointment to a prebend in Kildare Cathedral, given to him by his rector, who was bishop of that diocese, as well as Dean of Christ Church, and, for the last few years of his life, his duty at Monkstown was performed by the Rev. Daniel Dickinson who was for many years assistant curate of St. Werburgh's Church, in Dublin[71].

In 1742 Maddison was laid to rest under the Communion Table of his church, and was succeeded by the Rev. Thomas Heany, a scholar of Trinity College, who had been previously curate of St. Peter's Church, Dublin, and of Donnybrook. His promotion to Monkstown was due to the influence of Lord Chancellor Jocelyn, then just come to live at Mount Merrion, who possibly, sometimes attended Monkstown Church, and Heany, who enjoyed Jocelyn's friendship, through his marriage to a daughter of Walter Harris, expresses in his will his gratitude to his benefactor for securing him a position which brought him years of happiness[72]. During his time the church was enlarged by the erection of an aisle; and the provision, by the vestry, of a seat for the churchwardens, furnished with two large Prayer Books, and of a pair of stocks, are curiously significant of that age, Schools were established in the parish and, in 1767, the Rector, Dr. Jackson, Bishop of Kildare, preached on their behalf, and a collection, amounting to £70, was made, while, in the following year, a sum of £60 was obtained after a sermon from Dr. Young, Bishop of Leighlin[73].

Heany died in 1769, and was succeeded by the Rev. Thomas Robinson, afterwards Chancellor of Kildare Cathedral and Prebendary of St. Michael's, Dublin[74]. A second seat in the desk had been provided for an assistant curate,

---

[70] Diocesan Records; Matriculation Entry, Trinity College.

[71] Matriculation Entry, Trinity College; Cotton's "Fasti Ecclesiæ Hibernicæ;" Will of Alan Maddison; Hughes' "History of St. Werburgh's Church," p. 81.

[72] Diocesan Records; Will of Thomas Heany; Marriage Licence.

[73] Monkstown Vestry Book; *Exshaw's Magazine* for 1767, p. 591; *Dublin Journal*, No. 4337.

[74] See Hughes' "History of St. John's Church," p. 64.

and, in Heany's time, the Rev. Henry Wright, who died in 1773, at Carrickmines, then a well-known health resort, had acted in that capacity. He was succeeded by the Rev. Alexander La Nauze, who died in 1769 at his father's house in Dublin, greatly lamented, and the latter was followed by the Rev. John Andrews, the Rev. Isaac Ashe, afterwards a Vicar-Choral of Armagh Cathedral, and Rector of Tamlaght, and the Rev. Edward Beatty[75]. On Robinson's resignation, which took place in 1775, the Rev. John Hely was appointed to the perpetual curacy, and was succeeded in rapid succession by the Rev. Edward Ledwich, the Rev. John Forsayeth, a Fellow of Trinity College, and afterwards Archdeacon of Cork, and the Rev. William Jephson, who had previously held the dignity to which his predecessor was appointed[76]. A Roman Catholic Church, dedicated to St. Michael and St. Paul, existed in Monkstown at the close of the seventeenth century. In 1697 it was served by the Rev. Henry Talbot, and in 1704 by the Rev. Fergus Farrell. In 1766 the Rev. James Byrne, who was respected by his neighbours of all denominations, was the parish priest[77].

The Protestant population of the united parishes increased as the eighteenth century drew to a close. In 1762 the parishes of Stillorgan and Kilmacud had been severed from the others, and made into a separate charge, but, notwithstanding, the Church of Monkstown was, in 1777, found insufficient for the congregation. It was ruinous as well, and the parishioners were anxious that it should be pulled down and built on a more extensive plan. The graveyard afforded little accommodation for a larger church, and it was decided to change the site to that on which the present Church of Monkstown stands. In response to a petition, signed by, amongst others, Lords Ranelagh, Longford, and De Vesci; Mr. John Lees, of Newtown; Mr. John Mapas, of Rochestown, and Mr. Robert Byrne, of Cabinteely, the change was allowed by the Privy Council and, in 1785, the foundation stone of the new church was laid by His Excellency the Duke of Rutland (who subscribed £50 to the

---

[75] *Dublin Gazette*, No. 2627; *Pue's Occurrences*, vol. lxvi., No. 6860; Cotton's "Fasti Ecclesiæ Hibernicæ."

[76] See Cotton's "Fasti Ecclesiæ Hibernicæ," vol. ii., pp. 239, 247; Brady's "Records of Cork, Cloyne, and Ross," vol. i., p. 319, vol. ii., p. 433.

[77] D'Alton's "History of the County Dublin," p. 881; "Return of Roman Catholic Clergy in 1704;" Irish Parliament Records in Public Record Office.

fund for its erection), attended by the Archbishop of Cashel, the Bishop of Killala, the Right Hon. John Foster, then Chancellor of the Exchequer, and the Right Hon, John Beresford. Four years later, in 1789, it was consecrated by the Archbishop of Dublin, under the name of St. Mary's, and continued the parish church until superseded, about 1832, by the present grotesque structure. St. Mary's was considered in its day to be the finest church in Ireland, and contained, what was then thought, a good organ[78]. Dr. Jephson was succeeded, in 1791, as perpetual curate, by the Rev. John William Dudley Ryves, who was also Prebendary of St. Michael's in Christ Church Cathedral, and who is interred in the old churchyard of Killiney[79]; and Mr. Ryves was followed, in 1799, by the Rev. Marmaduke Cramer; in 1802, by the Rev. James Dunn; in 1804, by the Rev. Singleton Harpur; in 1815, by the Rev. Charles Lindsay, Archdeacon of Kildare; in 1855, by the Rev. William Fitzgerald, afterwards Bishop of Killaloe; in 1857, by the Rev. Ronald M'Donnell; in 1878, by the Rev. Joseph F. Peacocke, now Archbishop of Dublin, and in 1894, by the Rev. John C. Dowse.

St. Mary's Church, Monkstown, in 1793.
From a Plate in "The Sentimental and Masonic Magazine."

---

[78] Diocesan Records; *Hibernian Magazine* for 1785, p. 503; 1789, p. 502; 1800, p. 182; *Dublin Penny Journal,* vol. iii., p. 9.

[79] The following inscription appears on a flat stone, "Here lieth the remains of the Rev. Dudley Ryves, late Minister of the Parish of Monkstown and its Union, who departed this life March 2nd, 1801."

At the beginning of the nineteenth century the religious edifice, now known as Christ Church, Blackrock, was built, and opened as a Dissenting Chapel, by the Rev. Thomas Kelly, well-known as a writer of hymns, who was a son of the Right Hon. Thomas Kelly, one of the judges of the Common Pleas. Mr. Kelly was originally a member of the Established Church, but afterwards joined the Methodists, and founded a sect of his own, called the Kellyites. This sect was short-lived, and his chapel, which forms the transepts of the present church, was bought by trustees for the use of the Established Church. Of the subsequent ecclesiastical history of Monkstown, the division of the parish under the Established Church, and the erection of the numerous sacred edifices of the various denominations which now adorn the district, it is here impossible and unnecessary to treat[80].

---

[80] Crookshank's "History of Methodism in Ireland," vol. ii., pp. 67, 83, 205; Carroll's "Succession of the Clergy of St. Bride's," p. 53; *Hibernian Magazine* for 1801, p. 514; "Diary of Anne, Countess of Roden."

PARISH OF KILL-OF-THE-GRANGE.

(Formerly called Clonkeen—i.e., Cluain Caoin, the Beautiful Meadow.)

This parish is shown on the Down Survey made in 1657 as consisting of the Townlands of Kill of ye Grange, Deanes Grange, Rochestown, Ballintle, Lytle Newtowne, Cornettscourt, Killbegoge, and Stillorgan.

Kill of ye Grange is now represented by the Townland of Kill-of-the-Grange.

Deanes Grange is represented by Dean's Grange, Foxrock, and Galloping Green South, and by the small Townland of Waltersland in Stillorgan Parish.

Rochestown is represented by Rochestown Domain, Rochestown, Johnstown, and Woodpark.

Ballintle is represented by Ballinclea (*i.e.,* Baile an tsleibhe, the Town of the Mountain), Scalpwilliam, and Rocheshill.

Lytle Newtowne is represented by Newtown Park, Newpark, and Galloping Green North.

Cornettscourt is represented by Cornelscourt (*i.e.,* Corner's Court) and Cabinteely (*i.e.,* Caban-t-sighile, Sheela's cabin).

Killbegoge appears to be represented by part of the Townland of Kilbogget in Killiney Parish.

Stillorgan is now the Parish of Stillorgan.

The Townlands of Tipperstown (*i.e.,* Baile an tobair, the Town of the Well) and Mulchanstown, now included in Kill of the Grange Parish, are shown on the Down Survey as in Taney Parish, under the name of Tiberstown.

The objects of archæological interest in the parish are the ruined church of Kill of the Grange and its crosses and bullan stone.

Kill-of-the-Grange and Dean's Grange.

THESE villages derive from very early times, and were, 600 years ago, places of more importance than they are to-day. All that now exists to remind us that they have a history is the ruined church and the house called Kill

Abbey, which, though it has lost its original characteristics, bears the date 1595, and is surrounded by yew trees of extreme age. But in the early part of the last century there were extensive remains of mediæval buildings in the village of Dean's Grange[81].

These buildings stood in the centre of the property owned by the Augustinian Canons of the Priory of the Holy Trinity (the builders of Christ Church Cathedral, adjoining which their Priory stood), in the southern part of the County Dublin, and though probably not so strongly fortified, were similar to those belonging to the Cistercian Monks, at Monkstown. They comprised a house, to which the canons came for country air and for the transaction of the business of their estate, and numerous farm offices, in some cases only fragile structures of mud and wood, necessary for the cultivation of the large extent of land which the canons retained in their own hands as a home farm. Also, there was a village close by, containing thirty-five houses, known as the "Town of the Grange," in which lived their employees, including a bailiff, two smiths, a weaver and an officer called a Chamberlain.

The lands of Kill-of-the-Grange, which had been given to the Priory before the English Conquest by Donagh, son of Donald Grossus, and had been confirmed to that religious establishment by Archbishops, Popes, and Kings, had been brought, in spite of the raids of the Irish tribes, to which they were equally subject with those of Monkstown, into a high state of cultivation before the fourteenth century. They had been returned at the close of the preceding century as unable to bear taxation, but this was probably due to some incursions, more than usually severe in their results, which had then recently taken place. The tenants of the Priory, who were almost invariably bound to render service on the home farm, were, in the fourteenth century, prosperous and well-to-do, one or two being of sufficiently good position to join the Prior at table. Nine of them resided not far from the Priory buildings in the "Town of the Church," which corresponded with the village of Kill-of-the-Grange. There, also, the clerk of the church and two cottiers had houses. The peculiar properties of the soil close to that village, which have led in recent years to the establishment of brick and pottery works, were then known, and the sale of clay, for making earthenware, was a source of profit to the Priory.

---

[81] This information has been given to the author by the Rev. Maxwell H. Close, M.A., who recollects the remains.

As the lands of the Priory extended from Murphystown, at the foot of the Three Rock Mountain, to Killiney, at the sea, the business of the estate was very considerable. The Prior, like a layowner, exercised manorial jurisdiction over the tenants, and a court, presided over by the brother who held the office of seneschal, or land agent, was regularly held at Kill-of-the-Grange, to redress misdemeanours and nuisances, and to settle disputes of property. As well as civil, the Prior had military responsibilities, and was liable for the provision and equipment of a certain proportion of the county levy or militia. To the seneschal fell the duty of maintaining an efficient and sufficient number of the tenantry for that service, and of furnishing them with greaves, belts, and other requirements of war. The force was periodically inspected by an officer appointed by the Crown, whose visits to Kill-of-the-Grange, accompanied by many men of the regular army, were great events only exceeded in importance by those of the Archbishop of Dublin, who sometimes stayed in the Priory house with his retinue for several days at a time, on his way to and from Newcastle.

A vivid picture, with the most minute details, of life on the Priory farm is preserved for us in the Account Roll of the Priory, which has been edited with extraordinary care and ability by the present Deputy-Keeper of the Records in Ireland. In it we read of the live stock, of the crops, and of the farm implements; we make acquaintance with the canons, with the tenants, with the bailiff, who accounted—even to a peck—for the corn, and with the other farm servants; and we follow the agricultural operations throughout the year: the winter and spring sowing, in which fourteen ploughs, with twenty-eight men were engaged; the thinning and weeding of the crops, which required sixty-four labourers, and the harvest, in which as many as eighty-eight men on one day, and an average of thirty men for three weeks, took part. This army was fed by the canons, and when dinner hour came the bailiff, by a shrill blast from the horn which he constantly carried, summoned the weary workmen to partake of pork and herrings, and bread and ale; while in the Priory house the canons regaled their more important tenants and neighbours on mutton and pork, beef and poultry, herrings and eggs, and wine and ale, in unstinted quantities.

The dissolution of the Priory, in 1539, produced less change in its estates than that of other religious establishments, as it was immediately reconstituted as the Cathedral establishment of the Church of the Holy Trinity, commonly called Christ Church, the Prior becoming the first Dean, and the canons the first prebendaries of the Cathedral. In support of his dignity, the manor of Kill-of-the-Grange was granted to the Dean and the Priory House, at what was henceforth known as Dean's Grange, became his country residence. The demesne lands were let. A holding, containing land on the east side of the Church, and land near the Roman well, with a house, which probably became the chaplain's residence, and a flaxyard, were leased, in 1542, to the chaplain of the Church; and the lands and tithes of the manor, town, and fields of the Grange were leased, in 1561, to Christopher Bassenet, John Brady, and John Hore, then the chaplain[82].

Kill Abbey.
From a Photograph by Thomas Mason.

The house known as Kill Abbey was, doubtless, built in 1595, the date it bears, by George Ussher, a merchant of Dublin to whom was leased, in 1592,

---

[82] "Account Roll of the Priory of the Holy Trinity, Dublin," edited by James Mills, and published by the Royal Society of Antiquaries of Ireland; and Christ Church Deeds.

by the Chapter of the Cathedral, "the farm of Clonkeen, then commonly called the Kill." The curate's house, with its curtilage, which stood on these lands, was excepted, and besides a money rent it was agreed that there should be annual offerings of corn and hens, and the best beast on the death of the lessee. Ussher was succeeded by his sister, Rose, who had been twice married, first to John Money, sometime Mayor of Dublin, and secondly, to John Garvey, Archbishop of Armagh. On her death, which took place in 1612, she bequeathed the farm to the children of Walter Harold, but it does not seem to have long remained in their possession. A few years later, in 1623, Christopher Wolverston, of whose family we shall read under Stillorgan is returned as being the tenant for the Kill farm, and William Gilbert for the mensal lands[83].

The months of lawlessness, which succeeded the outbreak of the Rebellion, in October, 1641, were heavily felt in the Kill and at Dean's Grange. John Brackenbury, who is described as a resident of the latter place, deposed that during December and January the rebels made several descents on his farm, and carried off cattle and stock to a very considerable value, and, three days after Christmas, a party of the rebels came to the residence of the curate, the Rev. Joseph Smithson, at Kill, carried off his wife and her maid, and subsequently hanged them both at Powerscourt. Two months later, in February, 1642, a regiment comprising 1,000 men, under the command of Lord Lambart, who was created, some years later, Earl of Cayan, marched out to clear the southern side of Dublin of the rebels, and encountered the enemy in about equal numbers at Dean's Grange. The soldiers completely routed them, killing about 100 and taking fifteen prisoners. Amongst the latter, who only escaped death on the field to find it on the gallows, was a younger son of Mr. Walsh, of Clonmannon, in the County Wicklow, a gentleman by birth, though then presenting the appearance of a vagrant. The casualties of the army were returned as one killed and one wounded. Some weeks afterwards the stronghold of the rebels at Carrickmines was destroyed, but fugitives still wandered about the country and caused the peaceable inhabitants much alarm. In the month of May one of these fugitives came to the principal residence in Dean's Grange, and threatened "the good woman" of the house—accusing her of giving shelter to an English captain. She denied that

---

[83] Ball Wright's "Ussher Memoirs," pp. 35, 39; Christ Church Deeds.

she had done so, and told him that it would be better for him to follow his trade than rebellion. To this he replied, as a witness, who alleged that Brackenbury was in league with the rebels, relates, that he did not dare to show his head since he had been sent by his master, Brackenbury, with powder to the rebels at Carrickmines[84].

Towards the close of the Commonwealth period, Dean's Grange contained some fifteen houses, and had a population of eight English and sixty-one Irish. The chief house was occupied by Ralph and Nathaniel Swinfield, who held the lands, and who were succeeded by the Proud family, with whom some of the Swinfields intermarried. In Kill-of-the-Grange there were eight houses and a population of three English and twelve Irish. The widow of Christopher Merry, a Dublin baker, resided in the house built by George Ussher, and farmed the lands. On her death, the property passed to her granddaughter, who was twice married, first, to Thomas Fitzsimons, and secondly, to Walter Nangle[85]. In the beginning of the eighteenth century the Fitzsimons family, who succeeded to the house and lands found it convenient, owing to the operations of the Penal Laws, to assign them to Mr. William Espinasse, of Dublin, and he was subsequently accepted as tenant by the Cathedral. Espinasse was a descendant of a French family, which had emigrated to Ireland after the revocation of the Edict of Nantes, and had acquired much wealth in business. On his death, in 1740, he left a widow, "endowed with so many excellent qualities that to enumerate them would appear like flattery," and several children. His eldest son, Isaac, who succeeded him, was an officer in the Dragoons, and married, in 1754, a lady of beauty and fortune, the daughter of Richard Magennis, of the County Down. He resided at Kill Abbey for many years, becoming a magistrate, and serving as High Sheriff of the County Dublin, and was succeeded by his eldest son, Richard, whose representatives still occupy the house[86].

---

[84] "Depositions of 1641"; Borlase's "History of the Irish Rebellion," App., p. 114; Hickson's "Ireland in the Seventeenth Century," vol. ii., p. 26; "The Particular Relation of the Present Estate and Condition of Ireland," Lon. 1642, preserved in the National Library.

[85] "Census of 1659"; Hearth Money Roll; Fleetwood's Survey; Down Survey; Will of Christopher Merry

[86] Berry's "Pedigree of the Families of the County Kent," p. 333 Josiah Brown's "Reports of Cases in the High Court of Parliament," edited by Tomlins; vol. vii., p. 345; *Dublin Journal*, No. 2643; *Pue's Occurrences*, vol. li., No. 68.

ROCHESTOWN.

THE fine old mansion, known as Rochestown House, was evidently in former times the residence of some family of position, and indicated until lately by its high roof and pointed gables, that it was a structure of the early part of the eighteenth century. Near it there is a great gateway and remains of a stately drive, which show that the demesne was in keeping with the house. On the lawn, in front of the mansion, there is a fragment of a castle, similar to those which stood at Seapoint and elsewhere in the neighbourhood.

Rochestown House.
From a Photograph by Thomas Mason.

The lands appear to have been originally included under those of Dalkey, and were probably the lands of that place for which the Talbot family rendered annually to the Crown, in the thirteenth century, a goshawk, or its value, 6*s.* 8*d.*,—a substantial sum in those days. On account of their use for falconry, hawks were then much prized, especially Irish ones, and the goshawk was one of the largest birds used in the sport. Sometimes the value of the bird was paid, but the owner of Rochestown, in 1369, rendered his rent in kind, and had the effrontery to deliver a useless goshawk, for which he was fined by the Court of Exchequer. The tithes were paid to the Priory of the Holy Trinity, which was no less careful than the Crown to protect its rights, and employed an agent to see that the full amount of corn was delivered into its granary at Dean's Grange. About the middle of the sixteenth century, the lands, which were occupied by a son of the owner of Loughlinstown, James Goodman, and on which a castle then stood, were held by the Talbots of Belgard, under another branch of the family, described as of Rathdown, and, possibly, were "the castle and lordship of Yenah called Dalkey," which, in 1563, was assigned by Robert Talbot, of Belgard, to Matthew Birsell and Thomas Lawless[87].

At the beginning of the seventeenth century the lands of Rochestown, to which those of Scalpwilliam were joined, and on which there were, besides the castle, a number of houses and a wood of considerable extent, had come into the possession of John Fagan, of Bullock, who held them under the Talbots. They were probably assigned by him to Alderman Robert Kennedy, who, before his death, in 1624, had purchased them in fee. Kennedy was a friend of John Fagan's father, and owned much property in Dublin, including a celebrated mansion called Carberry House, in Skinner's-row, in which he resided. He left a number of sons, and strictly entailed his real estate on his heirs male, but in the troublous times the family became extinct in the male line, and Rochestown was claimed, on the Restoration, by Patrick Mapas, the son of his youngest daughter[88].

The Mapas family was of great antiquity in the County Louth where, in the fourteenth century, one of the name had been the victor of Edward Bruce. During the eighteenth century, first as Roman Catholics, and afterwards as Protestants, the owners of Rochestown occupied a leading place in the County of Dublin. Patrick Mapas, whose father was one of the first of the family to settle in Dublin, died while the claim to Rochestown

---

[87] "Hawks and Hounds in Ireland," by John P. Prendergast, and "The Norman Settlement in Leinster," by James Mills in *Journal, R. S. A. I.*, vol. ii., page 153, vol. xxiv., p. 173; Fiant Elizabeth, No. 266; Exchequer Inquisition, Philip and Mary, No. 13; Molyneux's "Collectanea de Rebus Hibernicis."

[88] Chancery Inquisitions, Jac. L, No, 19; Will of Alderman Robert Kennedy; Decrees of Innocents, iv., 56.

was before the court, but the proceedings were carried on by his widow, on behalf of their eldest son, Christopher, then a minor, and a decree was given in his favour. The occupant of the Castle, Matthew Boyce, Was obliged to vacate it, and the Mapases came to reside there. Soon afterwards, in 1674, Christopher Mapas made an alliance with the leading Roman Catholic family of the county, the Fitzwilliams of Merrion, by his marriage to a daughter of the third viscount, a lady who is said to have been "an extraordinary wife, mother, and family woman, most pious and truly charitable." In spite of the fact that his name and that of his brother, Lieutenant John Mapas, of Dongan's Dragoons, appear in a list of persons attainted by William III., Mapas contrived to retain his property, and was amongst the few Roman Catholics allowed to carry arms and to keep a sword, a case of pistols, and a gun. He was a gentleman of "the most worthy and honest character, and of unknown charity," and his death, which took place in 1719, caused great lamentations among the poor. His mother, who had married as her second husband, Mr. Edward Taylor, died a few years before her son, in 1711, leaving in her will a shilling to each poor widow in Rochestown, and in the neighbouring townlands; and his widow, the Hon. Rose Mapas, survived him until 1745, when she died at Rochestown, "in all the odour of sanctity," at a very advanced age.

Rochestown had undergone great improvements in the time of Christopher Mapas, and a modern house had been built; but the present one was probably erected by his eldest son, John Mapas, whose name, with the family arms, and the date 1750, it bears. To it were attached numerous offices, chief amongst these being a brewery and a pigeon-house, enclosed in a courtyard, and close by there were gardens, pleasure grounds, orchards, and a bowling green. John Mapas is said to have succeeded, on his father's death, to an estate of considerable value, and, like his father, made a good alliance, marrying a daughter of the seventh Baron of Louth. On his death, which took place in 1756, at his town house, in St. Stephen's-green, he was succeeded by his eldest son, Christopher. The latter, who resided abroad, died, in 1765, in Germany, and Rochestown then came into the possession of his eldest son, John Mapas, who had married, in 1757, a daughter of a successor in the title conferred on Sir Gerald Aylmer, of Monkstown. She died three years later, and the house was let to Mr. Edward Nicholson, M.P.

for Old Leighlin, who was connected by marriage with the Earls of Inchiquin[89].

A wood had existed at Rochestown from early times, as we have seen, and though clearances had been made round the house, which a contemporary writer condemns for its want of view, some fine trees still remained. Through their estate, which afforded attractive building sites, the Mapases made the existing roads, and other houses began to be built. The first of these was Granitefield, which was occupied for many years by Sir John Macartney, M.P. for Fore, who was knighted, and subsequently made a baronet, in recognition of his efforts to promote inland navigation in Ireland. In his time Granitefield was remarkable for its myrtles and arbutus trees, and for its vineries and hothouses. At Rochestown, which had a reputation as a health resort, the Right Hon. William Burton Conyngham, the great patron of Irish antiquities and art of his day, was staying, shortly before his death, in 1796, and there a gentleman, on calling to see him, found a battalion of physicians, surgeons, and apothecaries in attendance upon him[90].

Mr. Mapas, who soon returned to live at Rochestown House, married again—a Miss Wheatley, of Cheshire—and had by her an only surviving daughter. The latter married in 1789, Mr. Richard Wogan Talbot, who succeeded to the peerage of Talbot of Malahide, conferred upon his mother, and upon Mr. Mapas's death, in 1797, they became the owners of Rochestown House, which has undergone many vicissitudes during the last century.

---

[89] D'Alton's "King James's Irish Army List," p. 292; Hearth Money Roll; "History of St. Audoen's" in *The Irish Builder* for 1886 and 1887; "Ormonde Manuscripts," vol. ii., p. 479, published by the Historical Manuscripts Commission; *Pue's Occurrences,* Feb. 21-24, 1719; Wills of the Mapases; Funeral Entries in Ulster's Office; *Dublin Journal,* Nov. 10-14, 1741; *Exshaw's Magazine* for 1765, p. 708; Religious Returns of 1766. Lodge's "Peerage of Ireland," edited by Mervyn Archdall, vol. ii., p. 60.

[90] Wilson's "Topographical Description of Dalkey," in *Exshaw's Magazine* for 1770, p. 489; Post Chaise Companion, ed. 1786 "Rambles through Ireland," by a French Emigrant; *Hibernian Magazine,* 1801, p. 514.

Killiney Hill.

KILLINEY Hill stands in the townland of Mount Mapas, or Scalpwilliam. The lands of Scalpwilliam are first mentioned under that name in the beginning of the seventeenth century, and from that time followed the same devolutions of ownership as the Rochestown property. The obelisk, which stands on the summit of the hill and which is a very prominent object, was erected by Mr. John Mapas, in 1741, a year of scarcity and hardship, when fever and famine devastated Ireland. It bears the quaint inscription: "Last year being hard with the poor, the wall around these hills and this were elected by John Mapas, Esq. June, 1742."

About the same time a house had been built on or near the site of Killiney Castle. It contained considerable accommodation, and its sea and land prospect was accounted the finest in Ireland. Except towards the sea, "where nature had sufficiently enclosed them," the lands were surrounded by a stone wall and were estimated to contain some 150 acres. The house had been originally called Mount Mapas, but in 1755, was known as Roxborough. It was then in occupation of Captain Edward Maunsell, who served as High Sheriff of the County Dublin in that year. He had married a daughter of Philip Ridgate, LL.D., the widow of Mr. William Roberts, and on his death, which took place in 1765, in York-street, Dublin, left by her an only son. This son, Thomas Ridgate Maunsell, afterwards resided with his mother in Rochestown-avenue, and devoted much time to genealogical research, with the object of compiling a history of his family. Lead had been discovered on the lands of Roxborough, and mines had been, in 1751, opened, which, two years later, when a vein of great thickness was discovered, were reported to be in a most flourishing condition. They were closed a few years later, and a second attempt to work them in 1784 proved equally unsuccessful[91].

---

[91] *Dublin Journal,* No. 2665; Leases in Registry of Deeds Office; Wills of the Maunsells; *Exshaw's Magazine* for 1765, p. 64; Cole Manuscripts, British Museum, Add. MS. 5846, f. 67; *Dublin Journal,* No. 2717; Rutty's "Natural History of the County Dublin," vol. ii., p. 140; *Exshaw's Magazine* for 1784, p. 743.

Obelisk on Killiney Hill in 1795.
From a Plate drawn by F. Jukers

Before his death Captain Maunsell assigned his interest in Roxborough to Colonel the Hon. Henry Loftus, M.P. for Bannow, in the County Wexford, the central figure in one of the most protracted and keenly-contested legal struggles of the eighteenth century. He was a descendant of the great Archbishop Loftus, of Elizabeth's reign, and was younger son of Nicholas Loftus, of the County Wexford, who was created a peer as Baron Loftus and Viscount Loftus of Ely. His brother, who had succeeded to those titles on the death of their father, and who had in addition been created an earl, died in 1766, leaving an only son. This son, now the second earl, who was of extreme delicacy of constitution, and had been persistently neglected and ill-treated by his father, was taken by his uncle, Colonel Loftus, under his protection. Through his mother, a daughter of Sir Gustavus Hume, of the County Fermanagh, who had long pre-deceased her husband, the young earl was entitled to large property, and his mother's family had, before his father's death, instituted proceedings to prove that he was incapable of managing his affairs. His case was ably conducted by his uncle (it did not come on for trial until after his father's death), and the decision was in favour of the young earl's sanity. Three years later, in spite of every care on his uncle's part, the young man died, making a will, by which he bequeathed all his property to his uncle. His mother's relatives sought to have this will set aside, as obtained by undue influence, but were again unsuccessful, and Colonel Loftus succeeded to his nephew's estates, as well as to the barony and viscountcy. The pages of "Baratariana," where the colonel figures prominently as Count Henrico Loftonzo, allege that he deserted his old political friends to obtain a favourable decision from "the innocent Phil Tisdal," who was Judge of the Prerogative Court, as well as Attorney-General, and also tell of the efforts of his wife to secure Lord Townshend, then Lord Lieutenant, as husband for her niece, the lovely Dolly Monro, and Loftonzo's own intrigues to obtain an earldom, which was afterwards conferred on him[92].

Possessed with an unbounded passion for improvement, and a skill equal to that passion, as a contemporary writer says, Loftus converted the barren

---

[92] Josiah Brown's "Reports of Cases in the High Court of Parliament," vol. i., p. 450; vol. vii., p. 469; Prerogative Cause Papers, Ely *v.* Rochford, in Public Record Office; "Rathfarnham Castle; its sale and history," by John P. Prendergast, in *The Irish Times,* May 19, 1891; "Baratariana"; *Dublin Journal, * No. 4148.

hills and rocks round Roxborough, called by him Loftus Hill, into good meadow and pasture lands, frequently being obliged to blast the rock, and to draw earth to cover it, in order to obtain his object. Round the hill he cut the present road, and planted the west side with trees and shrubs. The house was a large one, but the offices were small. It was his intention to rebuild them, but this he did not accomplish, as in Rathfarnham Castle, the ancient seat of the family, which he repurchased for his nephew, and succeeded to himself, he found greater scope for the extravagant magnificence which is displayed in the classic gateway on the Dodder, constructed by him. After his succession to the titles Lord Loftus disposed of Loftus Hill; in 1778 it was occupied by Mr. Medlicott, and subsequently by Mr. Minchin[93].

The hill was, in 1790, taken by Lord Clonmell, with the intention of erecting a mansion there in place of his seat at Temple Hill, but his improvements ended in the construction of a park, at a cost of some £3,000 which, on its completion, he stocked with deer. Nearly 200 men were employed by him at one time in that work, and in making roads and planting. A tourist in 1796 describes a handsome banqueting hall, which was built by Colonel Loftus, and mentions that, in addition to the obelisk, which Lord Clonmell had restored, a memorial was about to be placed on the hill, in pursuance of the will of the last Mr. Mapas, who left a large sum for the erection of a monument to his family. During the last century the neighbourhood was much developed by Mr. Robert Warren, of Killiney Castle, whose name, as its restorer in 1840, the obelisk bears, and the hill having been purchased for a park, was, in 1887, opened and dedicated to the public use by the late Prince Albert Victor of Wales, in memory of Queen Victoria's Jubilee[94].

BALLINCLEA.

THE lands of Ballinclea, or the Town of the Mountain, are first mentioned in the time of the Commonwealth. They were then forfeited lands, and had belonged to the owner of Loughlinstown, James Goodman, who had

---

[93] Wilson's "Topographical Description of Dalkey," in *Exshaw's Magazine* for 1770, p. 469; Taylor and Skinner's Maps of Ireland; Post Chaise Companion, ed. 1786.

[94] *Dublin Chronicle* for 1790-1791, p. 671 Ferrar's "View of Dublin," p. 77.

mortgaged them to his cousin, Rowland Goodman. The tithes were paid to the Cathedral of Christ Church, as they had, no doubt, been in mediæval times to the Priory of the Holy Trinity. After the Restoration the lands, on which there were two houses and a population of nine Irish, were granted, amongst much other property, to the Duke of York, afterwards James II., and remained in his possession until his abdication. Some years after that event, in 1703, they were put up for auction by the trustees of the forfeited estates, and sold to Mr. Samuel Jackson. They became subsequently the property of Sir Oliver Crofton, Bart, whose baronetcy, conferred on an ancestor after the Restoration, became extinct on his death. Crofton was a rollicking blade, and did not bear the most immaculate character. In early life he had stood his trial for killing a man, one of the Massys of Duntrileague, in a duel, and his proceedings, after the death of his predecessor in the title, had not been to his credit. Attempts were made from time to time to induce people to build on the excellent sites which the lands of Ballinclea afforded, and finally Crofton came to live there himself. Loftus, whose lands adjoined, found Crofton a most unpleasant neighbour, and, on his boundary wall being thrown down by Crofton and his servants, sought, in 1765, the protection of the House of Commons. The House found that a breach of privilege had been committed, and some of Crofton's servants, who had insulted Loftus, were taken into custody. The fine mansion which now stands on the lands was built, in the last century, by the Talbots of Malahide, and is still occupied by members of the family[95].

CABINTEELY.

NOT far from the village of Cabinteely, or Sheela's Cabin, on the road to Stillorgan, there are a few cottages known by the name of Cornelscourt, near which, until recently, were to be seen the ruins of a castle. In the opinion of Austin Cooper, who visited the ruins in 1781, and who found the arched vault entire, though the upper storey was open and ruinous, the castle had been a

---

[95] Fleetwood's Survey; Census of 1659; Certificate for Adventurers and Soldiers i., 58; Book of Postings and Sale; *Pue's Occurrences,* vol. xl., No. 49, vol. lx., No. 9; *Dublin Journal,* Nos. 2026, 2522 Journals of the Irish House of Commons.

mean one, and it is stated in one of the Commonwealth surveys that the roof was of thatch[96].

The lands which surrounded the castle, including those new designated as Cabinteely, were, in the fourteenth century, known as the lands of Cornelscourt, and are mentioned in a rental of the Priory of the Holy Trinity as belonging to that establishment, and as held by Gregory Taunton, one of the chief tenants in its manor of Kill-of-the-Grange. Before the dissolution of the religious houses the lands had become the property of the Abbey of Lismullen, in the County Meath, a nunnery of the Augustinian Order, like the Priory—a fact which may have had some connection with their transfer to it, and, in 1539, the Abbess, Mary Cusack, surrendered them to the Crown. The lands, which contained besides the Castle, a tower and eight cottages, and were partly covered by moor and underwood, were then leased to Sir Thomas Cusack, afterwards Lord Chancellor of Ireland, and probably a relation of the Abbess, but his lease was soon broken, and, in 1545, they were granted by the Crown, with those of Monkstown, to Sir John Travers. After Travers' death they passed, like the latter, first to the Eustace, and afterwards to the Cheevers family. In 1597 a priest called Thomas Kean, *alias* Cahill, was resident at Cornelscourt, and possibly there was then a small chapel on the lands. On Walter Cheevers being transplanted to Connaught, the Parliament gave Cornelscourt to William Morgan, described as a gentleman. The Castle, with its thatched roof, was then in good repair, and, at the close of the Commonwealth period, there were five English and twenty-seven Irish inhabitants occupying eight houses on the lands. After the Restoration Cornelscourt, with Monkstown and his other property, was restored to Walter Cheevers, and descended from him to the Byrnes, who owned the lands until recently[97].

The family of Byrne, or O'Byrne, which, on Cheevers' death, became identified with Cornelscourt, and afterwards with Cabinteely, was, in early times, one of the most powerful and distinguished in Leinster, and numbered amongst its members two of the most remarkable of the ancient Irish kings.

---

[96] Cooper's Note Book.

[97] "Account Roll of the Priory of the Holy Trinity," p. 194; Exchequer Inquisition Co. Dublin, Hen. VIII., No. 186; Fiants, Henry VIII., No. 91; Elizabeth No. 6200; Census of 1659; Hearth Money Roll.

John Byrne, who married the only surviving daughter of Walter Cheevers, was a direct descendant of one of these, and was himself a man of good position. He had served as High Sheriff of the County Wicklow, and his brother, an ancestor of the Barons de Tabley, had been created a baronet. His eldest son, Walter, who was an infant at the time of his death, and who married in after years a daughter of Mr. Christopher Mapas, of Rochestown, succeeded to the ownership of Cornelscourt, but he left no issue. On his death, in 1731, his property passed to his younger brother, John, who had been born after their father's death, and this John Byrne was succeeded by his eldest son, George. In their time the seat of the family was changed from Cornelscourt to Cabinteely, and a modern house which, under the name of Cabinteely House, was long occupied by their successors, was built on the site of the one now known as Marlfield. George Byrne married a cousin of Robert Nugent, a well-known English politician of that day, who was created a peer as Viscount Clare and Earl Nugent. The latter has been described as a jovial and voluptuous Irishman, and, for reasons which need not be stated here, was a generous patron to his cousin's family[98].

The present Cabinteely House, in his time known as Clare Hill, which Nugent built on the Byrnes' lands and bequeathed to them, was not the least splendid amongst his princely gifts. It is a large and handsome mansion, forming three sides of a square, and, in its well-proportioned and finely decorated reception-rooms, displays the cultured taste of its builder. Nugent probably occupied it but little. Shortly before his death, in 1788, he came to Ireland, in order to be near his daughter, the Marchioness of Buckingham, whose husband was then Lord Lieutenant, and Clare Hill was stated to be preparing for his reception, but he appears to have spent the few remaining months of his life in Dublin. George Byrne had died at Cabinteely, in 1763, when his children were still very young, and he was succeeded successively by his eldest son, Michael, a young man of great accomplishments, acquired at Eton and Oxford, who became a member of the English Parliament, as representative of Nugent's pocket-borough of St. Mawes, in Cornwall, and who died at Cabinteely, in 1772; by his second son, Gregory, remarkable for his charitable and kindly disposition, who died at Knightsbridge, in London,

---

[98] "Pedigree of the Byrnes," by G. D. Burtchaell in *The Irish Builder* for 1887, pp. 114, 288; "Memoirs of Robert, Earl Nugent," by Claud Nugent.

in 1774; and by his third son, Robert. The latter, who resided abroad, died, in 1799, at Lisbon, leaving a widow and three daughters—amiable and talented ladies, who succeeded to the property. Before 1794, Marlfield had been let to Mr. John Dwyer, "a solicitor of great eminence," who filled the position of Secretary to Lord Chancellor Clare and Lord Chancellor Redesdale. He rebuilt the house, which was occupied by him for many years, and on his death it passed into the possession of its present owners, the Jessops. Johnstown was the only other house of any importance in the neighbourhood at the close of the eighteenth century. In 1778 it was occupied by Mr. Love Hiatt, and, later on, by Mr. Williams[99].

TIPPERSTOWN.

THE lands of Tipperstown, or the Town of the Well, on which the Vartry Reservoirs are situated, formed portion of the property of the Priory of the Holy Trinity, and were included in the Manor of Kill-of-the-Grange. They were always occupied by tenants, and the leases, by the stringency of their provisions, rival in legal skill the work of the best lawyers of the present day. The tenant was bound to render service on the home farm at the winter and spring sowing and at harvest, to give to the Priory a portion of the beer which he brewed, to litigate in the Manor Court, and to aid the lessors in counsel, service, and assistance at any place within the County Dublin. Amongst the tenants in the thirteenth and fourteenth centuries were the families of Wyte, Hacket, Wythir, Harold, and Lagthenan. After the dissolution of the Priory these lands were leased, with those of Kill-of-the-Grange, in 1561, to Bassenet, Brady, and Hore, and, in 1591, being then described as "Ballitubbred, *alias* Waltersland, and the Moor of Leperstown," to Walter Harold, of Dublin. In 1623 they were held by William Wolverston, the owner of Stillorgan, and, in 1645, were in the occupation of Richard Swinfield, of Murphystown,

---

[99] *Dublin Chronicle,* 1788-1789, pp. 24, 64, 576, 632; O'Keeffe's "Recollections of his Life," vol. i., p. 294; *Dublin Gazelle,* Nos. 2561, 2562, 2564, 2862; Gaskin's "Irish Varieties," p. 201; Tyner's "Traveller's Guide through Ireland"; *Dublin Chronicle,* 1789-1790, p. 170; "Personal Recollections of Lord Cloncurry," p. 222; Monkstown Parish Register; *Dublin Chronicle,* 1790-1791, p. 720; *Hibernian Magazine* for 1801, p. 514.

doubtless a relative of the Swinfields, of Dean's Grange, who then deposed that he had been robbed by the rebels. After the Restoration the lands were recovered for the Chapter, by the energy of one of its members, Dr. Lightburne, from an alleged tenancy of Sir Henry Talbot, of Templeogue, and were, in 1664, leased to Robert Mossom, Master in Chancery, son of the Bishop of Derry of that name, and father of the Dean of Ossory, who was a friend of Swift's. They were subsequently leased, in 1724, to Christopher Ussher, of Booterstown, and afterwards of Mount Ussher, in the County Wicklow, Secretary of the Linen Board, "a very sensible, plain, good-natured man," according to Mrs. Delany, "with a meek little wife, who never made or marred sport." At the time of the Union they belonged to Councillor O'Farrell, and were farmed by him with great skill[100].

NEWTOWNPARK.

THESE lands, originally known as Newtown Little, are first mentioned at the time of the dissolution of the religious houses, and there is reason to think were then the site of an ancient chapel. The care of their spiritualities was given to the Dean of Christ Church, and their tithes were leased by the Chapter, in 1564, to Nicholas Cor, chaplain, and Gerald Long, a yeoman, of Simonscourt. In the sixteenth century the lands, on which there was a good slated house, were in the possession of the owners of Stillorgan, and were occupied by members of the Wolverston family. They continued in their possession during the next century, Francis Wolverston being in occupation of them before the Commonwealth, and James Wolverston, then owner of Stillorgan, being confirmed in their possession after the Restoration. At that time James Brackenbury, possibly a son of the Dean's Grange resident, was living in the house, which was subsequently occupied by James Reyly, who contributed to the subsidy assessment "in goods," and was probably a shopkeeper. As the eighteenth century advanced, villas were built, and the lands became populated. The village of Galloping Green, through which what was then the

---

[100] Christ Church Deeds; "Account Roll of the Priory of the Holy Trinity," p. 207; Depositions of 1641; Certificates of Innocents i., 6; *Notes and Queries,* 1st Ser. v., p. 176; Ball Wright's "Ussher Memoirs," p. 185 Archer's "Survey of the County Dublin."

high road from Dublin to Bray passed, became well known, and we are reminded of the fashions of the times by a highway robbery committed there, in 1751, by three servants, "with their hair turned up under their hats." It was announced, in 1787, that the famous Donnybrook Fair was to be removed to its neighbourhood, but the rumour proved to have no foundation[101]. Towards the close of that century Newtown Park had several residents of note, including Alexander Crookshank, M.P. for Belfast, and afterwards, from 1783 to 1800, a judge of the Common Pleas, whose death, in 1813, is recorded on a tablet in Monkstown Church[102]; the Hon. Joseph Hewitt, son of Lord Chancellor Lifford, then residing at Stillorgan, who was Crookshank's successor in the representation of Belfast, and a judge of the King's Bench for three short years before his death, in 1794[103]; Mr. Timothy Dyton, the printer of the *Dublin Gazette*, who died in 1796; and Dyton's son-in-law, Mr. St. George O'Kelly, High Sheriff, in 1794, of the County Dublin[104].

ECCLESIASTICAL HISTORY.

THE ruined church near the village of Kill-of-the-Grange is considered by archæologists to be of extreme antiquity. It consisted originally of the simple oblong which now forms the nave, and in which a primitive square-headed doorway, afterwards superseded by a round-headed one, and window are to

---

[101] Christ Church Deeds, Nos. 431, 1296; Carte Papers; Decrees of Innocents, iv. 194; Hearth Money Roll: Subsidy Roll; Down Survey; *Dublin Journal*, No. 2574; *Dublin Chronicle*, 1787-4788, p. 376.

[102] It bears the following inscription, "Sacred to the Memory of Alexander Crookshank, late of the City of Dublin, Esq.; he filled the situation of a Judge of the Court of Common Pleas in Ireland for seventeen years with ability and integrity; as it pleased God to give him a long life, so did He render it useful; his afflicted widow and children, who knew him best, have erected this small but sincere tribute to the memory of his departed worth; he died the 10th day of December. 1813, aged 77 years." Judge Crookshank was buried in Monkstown Graveyard, where a tomb records the date of his death, and that of his wife on February 1st, 1826, aged 79 years.

[103] Watson's Almanac; Smyth's "Law Officers of Ireland," and "Falkland's Review of the Irish House of Commons," p. 35.

[104] *Hibernian Magazine* for 1796, pt. ii., p. 96; *Dublin Chronicle*, 1790-1791, p. 200.

be seen. Its dimensions are, Mr. Wakeman says, the same as those of the building at Glendalough, known as St. Kevin's Kitchen. To this primitive church was added, in later times, the chancel, which was connected with the nave by means of an arch broken through its east wall, and the belfry erected on the western wall. Near the church there are the remains of two crosses and, in the grounds of Kill Abbey, close by, there is a stone with hollows, known to antiquaries as a bullan stone, and supposed to be of early Christian, if not of Pagan origin; also a sacred well—probably the one known in mediæval times as the Roman Well[105].

Ruined Church of Kill-of-the-Grange.
From a Photograph in the collection of the Royal Society of Antiquaries of Ireland.

The Church of Clonkeen was dedicated to St. Fintain, the priest who, doubtless, selected Kill-of-the-Grange as the scene of his evangelising efforts, and who is supposed to have flourished about the same time as St. Mochonna.

---

[105] "Primitive Churches in the County Dublin," by W. F. Wakeman in Journal *R. S. A. I.*, vol. xxi., pp. 405, 702; also see vol. xxvi., p. 405; *Irish Literary Gazette*, vol. iii., pp. 4, 9; *Proceedings of the Royal Academy*, vol. viii. ,pp. 62, 283, 3rd Ser, i. ,p. 257; "Leacs and Crosses of the Half Barony of Rathdown," by P. J. O'Reilly, *Journal R.S.A.I.*, vol. xxxi., pp. 144, 251.

After the English Conquest it was granted by the Pope to the Priory of the Holy Trinity, but, as we have seen, at the beginning of the thirteenth century, it formed, with the Chapel of Carrickbrennan and the Church of Dalkey, a prebend in St. Patrick's Cathedral. Before 1230 it was exchanged by the Chapter of St. Patrick's for the Church of Ballymore, and became the absolute property of the Priory, which constituted it a mother church, with the chapels of Carrickbrennan and Stillorgan appendant. It was, doubtless, served by one of the monks and, although, in 1294, returned as unable to bear taxation, was, in 1306, valued at £18 3*s*. 4*d*.

West Doorway of the Ruined Church of Kill-of-the-Grange.
From a Photograph in collection of the Royal Society of Antiquaries of Ireland.

There was constant litigation as to the right of the Archdeacon of Dublin to visit and exact fees from the churches of the Priory, and Kill-of-the-Grange was one of those in dispute. On the establishment of the Cathedral of Christ Church, the Church of Kill-of-the-Grange was assigned to the Dean as portion of his dignity, and was served by vicars appointed by him. Amongst these were, in 1542, John Callan, and, in 1561, John Here. The appointment of the vicar gave rise, in 1552, to litigation between the parishioners and the Dean, but the latter's right to the patronage was established by the Ecclesiastical Court. At the beginning of the seventeenth century, in 1615, the church, then in good repair, was served, with that of Dalkey, by "a reading minister," the Rev. Owen Ellis, and some years later, in 1630, when it had been unroofed by recent storms, by the Rev. Simon Swayne, the Vicar of Bray. Although the Dean received some £80 a year in tithes from the parish, Swayne's stipend was only £7, and as there was a congregation of twenty-four, the cure was not without its duties. To Swayne succeeded, in 1638, the Rev. Joseph Smithson, who valued the living at £40, and who was forced to flee to Dublin, with his two sons after his wife's abduction, and "exposed to great want and misery"; and, in 1643, the Rev. John Armistead, M.A., a minor canon, of St. Patrick's Cathedral, and afterwards vicar of Balscaddan. During the Comonwealth the church was reported to be ruinous, and it was never again used for service. There was probably a concealed Roman Catholic Church in the parish in the seventeenth and eighteenth centuries. In 1697, the Rev. Henry Talbot, who lived at Rochestown, was stated to be parish priest of Cabinteely, and, in 1704, the Rev. Richard Murphy was returned as parish priest of Kill[106].

---

[106] O'Hanlon's "Lives of the Irish Saints," vol. iii., p. 196; Christ Church Deeds; Mason's "History of St. Patrick's Cathedral," pp. 40, lxiv.; Regal Visitation of 1615; Archbishop Bulkeley's Report; Diocesan Records; Depositions of 1641; D'Alton's "History of the County Dublin," p. 881; "Return of Roman Catholic Clergy in 1704."

Ruined Castle at Dalkey.
From a Drawing by W. F. Wakeman.

PARISH OF DALKEY.

This parish which in the seventeenth century was included in the barony of Newcastle consists of the townlands of Dalkey and Dalkey Commons, together with Dalkey Island, Lamb Island, Maiden Rock, The Muglins, and Clare Rock.

It contains the following objects of archæological interest:—The Castles and ruined Church of Dalkey, and the ruined Church on Dalkey Island.

THE TOWN OF DALKEY.

THE modern Dalkey occupies the site of a fortified town, which began to decay some 400 years ago. Its port was, in mediæval times, not only the Kingstown of that age for travellers, but also the place of disembarkation for merchandise coming to Dublin, and the ancient town, which contained seven strong castles, was used as a safe place of storage for the goods until the merchants found it convenient to remove them to Dublin. Only two of the seven Castles now remain—one forms portion of Dalkey Town Hall; the other is a fairly complete ruin. They were inspected by Mr. J. H. Parker, C.B., at the same time as Bullock Castle, and are, in his opinion, buildings of the same era. He describes the one since converted to the use of a Town Hall as a plain square tower-house, or castle, with a solid parapet, and small windows. At the south-west corner a staircase is corbelled out, and on the north side there is a garderobe turret, while from the parapet a chimney and small bartizan project. The second castle, then in the same condition as at present, he describes as similar to its companion; but, from the fact that its battlement is in the form of steps, he considered it to be a building of somewhat later date. It is provided with a staircase, which is carried through the vaulted lower storey in the thickness of the wall, and then leads into an octagonal turret, and, in the upper room, there is a fireplace and garderobe[107].

---

[107] "Observations on the Ancient Domestic Architecture of Ireland," in *Archæologia*, vol. xxxviii., p. 162.

The Town by Hall of Dalkey.
From a Drawing by W. F. Wakeman.

Dalkey has a history, like Bullock, before its castles were built, and, until the beginning of the nineteenth century, rock monuments, dating from the time of the primitive inhabitants, were to be seen near the town. One of these, a cromlech, surrounded by a circle of upright stones, stood upon Dalkey Common; the other a great rock, known as Cloch Tobair Gailline, or the Rock of the Well of Gailline, overhung a sacred well on the top of Dalkey Hill. During the eighth century Dalkey was the scene of a battle between two Irish tribes, and Forgartach, son of Niall, King of Ireland, fell by the hand of Cinœth, son of Ingalach, on its plain. Doubtless the Danish invaders frequently landed at its port, and by them the Irish name of the place Delginis, or Thorn Island, was changed to Dalkey, which is Scandinavian in its origin. The English disembarked, so far as is known, near Waterford and Wexford, but, in 1171, while the Irish were besieging them in Dublin, a detachment of the Irish force was stationed at Dalkey, to guard its port, where the Irish expected their Danish allies to land. After the Conquest, Dalkey was granted, by Henry II., to Hugh de Lacy, Constable of Dublin, but was soon given by the latter to the See of Dublin. The Archbishops proved themselves worthy of the trust, and, under them, the town rapidly developed. The right to hold a market in Dalkey every Wednesday, and a fair on the Feast of St. Begnet, the patron saint of the place, was granted to them, and, at the same time, power was given to them to levy tolls, to be applied to the improvement of the walls of the town and the harbour, similar to those enforced in Dublin. Subsequently, a fair, which had been held at Powerscourt, was transferred there. The town was ruled by a provost and bailiffs, who had also authority over the port, and who were sometimes appointed by the Archbishop, and sometimes by the Crown. As regards the inhabitants, information is but meagre, and is only derived from the records of the Priory of the Holy Trinity, which had charge of the spiritualities of Dalkey, and owned some property in the town. In 1326, John Kendal, who supplied the Priory House at Kill-of-the-Grange with fish, was the tenant of the Priory at Dalkey, and a holding at Dalkey on the west side of the church, "looking from the sanctuary," which was given, in 1320, by Alice, wife of John de Dundrum, to Andrew FitzRichard, on his marriage to her daughter, as well as premises surrendered, in 1394, by Nicholas Pyn, and others leased, in 1439, by John Talbot, Lord of Feltrim, probably became portion of its property[108].

---

[108] *The Dublin Penny Journal,* vol. ii., p. 308; "Annals of the Four Masters;" Orpen's "Dermot and the Earl," p. 131; D'Alton's "History of the County Dublin, p. 887; Archbishop Alan's "Liber Niger"; Christ Church Deeds.

Cloth Tobair Gailline in 1776.
From a Drawing by Gabriel Beranger.

The port of Dalkey became more and more used as ships increased in size, and found the navigation of the Liffey impossible. To its port was consigned, in 1244, a cargo of deer, to stock the Royal park, at Glencree, and at its port, in 1303 and 1323, ships to convey reinforcements, and arms, and provisions for the expeditions against Scotland, were ordered to assemble. In legal proceedings, with respect to duty on wines, in 1305, it was proved that ships were obliged to discharge portion of their cargo at Dalkey, before attempting to cross the bar of Dublin, and, in 1306, it was found that wine for the King, which proved of inferior quality, had been landed there from Bordeaux, and re-shipped to Skinburness, in Cumberland—a port much used during the Scottish wars—and that to this circumstance, entailing a prolonged voyage on stormy seas from Michaelmas to Epiphany, the deterioration of the wine was due. Travellers of high position were constantly arriving and departing. In 1359, the officials of Dalkey were ordered to allow a Spanish ship to depart, which had been detained for the conveyance of the Prior of the Priory of St. John of Jerusalem, who was then Lord Chancellor of Ireland. In 1384, John Penros landed at Dalkey, on his arrival as Chief Justice of Ireland, a position from which he was afterwards promoted to the English Bench. In the following year Philip de Courtenay, Lord Deputy of Ireland, disembarked there, as did two years later Sir John de Stanley, an ancestor of the Earls of Derby, who was appointed Lieutenant of the Marquis of Dublin. In 1414, Sir John Talbot, Lord of Furnival, and afterwards Earl of Shrewsbury, landed there on his arrival as Lord Lieutenant. In 1427 and 1431, James Cornwalsh, Chief Baron of the Exchequer, who was "barbarously and cruelly" murdered in the Castle of Baggotrath, landed there, after spending, on both occasions, six months in England, on business of the State. And, in 1488, Sir Richard Edgecombe, after he had accepted homage on behalf of the King from the adherents of the pretender, Lambert Simnel, sailed from Dalkey, having been escorted from Dublin by the Archbishop, judges, and nobility. The constant passenger traffic had disadvantages as well as advantages. A pestilence, which devastated Ireland in the fourteenth century—killing, in Dublin alone, in four months, 14,000 persons—is said to have broken out at Dalkey, whither it was conveyed by some passenger from the Sister Isle, and, doubtless, almost depopulated the town[109].

During the fifteenth and sixteenth centuries, Dalkey rose to its greatest importance. It was able to contribute 200 men at arms to the county levy, and, in addition to weekly markets, seven fairs were annually held. To a traveller coming over Killiney Hill on a fine summer's day, a pretty picture then presented itself, as the town, with its busy port, broke upon his view. Its walls, its castles, and its church stood out clearly in the sunlight, and beneath them the blue water in the sound crowded with shipping. It is one of the fair days, and as the traveller enters the town he finds himself in an animated scene. The streets are crowded with persons intent on business. Here is a Chester merchant, just arrived with produce from the English markets, anxious to sell; there is one of his Dublin brethren equally anxious to buy. Along the causeway from the sea carts continually arrive, laden with merchandise to await in the Castles convenient transport to Dublin, and from a bark which has just entered the offing, there hurries on horseback a messenger of State, with despatches for the Lord-Deputy, while several other passengers follow.

---

[109] Sweetman's "Calendar of Documents relating to Ireland," 1171-1251, No. 2671, 1302-1307, No. 431; Patent and Close-Rolls; D'Alton's "History of the County Dublin," p. 888; Gaskins' "Irish Varieties," p, 29.

The records of the Priory of the Holy Trinity continue to afford information about the town. At the beginning of the sixteenth century, the Priory received from Johanna Waring, widow of Peter Bartholomew, and their daughter, gifts of land, and from James White, Chaplain of Dalkey, and Archdeacon of Armagh, a house within the town. In the latter half of the century the Chapter of the Cathedral, as the Priory establishment had then become, leased various premises, including eight houses, to Henry Walsh, of Suttonstown, who assigned them subsequently to Alderman Walter Ball, of Dublin, and a holding on the west side of the church to Thomas Morgan, who undertook to build a thatched house and to supply the Dean, when in residence at Dean's Grange, with fish. St. Mary's Abbey had also property in Dalkey, which, after the dissolution of that house, came, like Bullock, into the possession of Peter Talbot, of Fassaroe. Travellers still continued to use the port, and it was the one generally chosen by the chief governors. In 1534, Sir William Skeffington; in 1548, Sir Edward Bellingham; in 1553, Sir Anthony St. Leger; in 1565, Sir Henry Sidney, whose crossing was delayed for two months by contrary winds, in 1584 Sir John Perrot, and in 1599 the Earl of Essex, landed there; while in 1558 the Earl Of Sussex selected it as the place of embarkation for the expedition against the Scottish invaders in Ulster. It was also still used for merchandise, and, in 1559, the Master of the Rolls, who engaged in the manufacture of hats and tapestry, was allowed to export wool from the port of Dalkey, in exchange for the materials he required for "these mysteries"[110].

The close of the sixteenth century marks the disuse of Dalkey, and the adoption of Ringsend as the port of Dublin, and from that time the town lost its importance commercially, and soon became ruinous. The principal residents then were the Morgans and the Dongans. The latter were ancestors of the Earl of Limerick, who was attainted by William III., and were sons of John Dongan, Remembrancer of the Exchequer, who was leased, in 1586, by the Chapter of Christ Church Cathedral, a moiety of a castle in Dalkey. Later

---

[110] D'Alton's "History of the County Dublin," p. 889; Christ Church Deeds; "Chartularies of St. Mary's Abbey," vol. ii., p. 64; Exchequer Inquisition, Co. Dublin Philip and Mary, No. 8; Liber Munerum; Gaskins' "Irish Varieties"; Harris' "History Of Dublin," p. 35; "Communication between London and Dublin," in *The Irish Builder* for 1897, p. 48; Fiants, Elizabeth, No. 92.

on Sir John Dongan, a grandson of the Remembrancer, and Henry Walsh, were the chief inhabitants. Amongst other owners of property were the family of Barnewall of Shankill; of Fagan of Bullock, who succeeded to Talbot's property; of Bee, and of Kernan. In the time of the Commonwealth only one of the seven castles was habitable, and the population was returned as three English and forty-one Irish, inhabiting thirteen houses. Captain Richard Newcomen, who has been mentioned in connection with Bullock, was then the owner, but after the Restoration, besides Christ Church Cathedral, we find the Fagans, the Walshes, the Dongans, and the Wolverstons of Stillorgan, who had succeeded to the property of the Barnewalls, in possession. Subsequently, the Duke of York, afterwards James II., Viscount Fitzwilliam, and Sir Henry Talbot acquired property in the town[111].

At the beginning of the eighteenth century, on the sale of the Irish estates of James II., the possessions of that sovereign at Dalkey were bought by Colonel Allen, of Stillorgan, now represented by the Earl of Carysfort. Some years later, Eustace Budgell, one of the writers in the *Spectator,* was a resident at Dalkey. He was a cousin of Joseph Addison, under whose wing he came to Ireland, where he was appointed Under-Secretary of State, and, subsequently, Accountant-General, with a seat in Parliament, as member for Mullingar, a position which he held for only a few years. About the middle of that century the owners of Dalkey were Mr. Bull, Sir William Mayne, afterwards Baron Newhaven, son-in-law of the second Viscount Allen; and Mr. Baldwin, who held under Christ Church. Amongst the residents was Mr. Peter Wilson, a well-known bookseller, and publisher of the Dublin *Almanac* or *Directory* of his day, who wrote a charming description of Dalkey and its neighbourhood, to which reference has already been made. He says that, in the year 1770, the town comprised, besides the venerable ruins of the castles and of the church, some good houses, and about twenty cabins, which "served indiscriminately for the owners, their cattle, and their swine." Within his recollection the street, owing to its rocky surface, had been impassable for carriages, and difficult for a horse to traverse, but it had been levelled, and the old road which ran on the

---

[111] "Description of Ireland in 1598," ed. by Rev. Edmund Hogan, p. 37; Chancery Inquisition Co. Dublin, Car. I., Nos. 12, 19; "Calendar of Patent Rolls James I.," p. 217; Down Survey; Census of 1659; Hearth Money Roll; Decrees of Innocents, ii., 122, iii., 138, i., 18, iv., 194; Certificates for Adventurers and Soldiers, i., 58, x., 514.

north side of the town was then only used on the occasion of funerals. Of the castles, six, which were known as the Goat's Castle (now forming part of the Town Hall); the House Castle, the Black Castle, Wolverston's Castle, Dongan's Castle, and Archbold's Castle, remained. The House Castle had been converted into a dwelling by Mr. Robert Barry; the Black Castle had been made into a billiard-room; two more were inhabited by publicans; the fifth was a stable, and the sixth formed part of a cottage. The lead mines on the lands of Rochestown had been originally worked by a firm, which had its smelting houses on Dalkey Common. These had been sold, in 1757, after some hundred tons of lead ore had been raised, and were reopened, about the year 1780, by Messrs. Darcy and Knox, but were soon again in the market. A cotton factory, which, in 1781, was totally destroyed by fire, had also been established in the town, on ground belonging to Mr. Watson, of Bullock.

At the close of the eighteenth century, the principal inhabitants were Sir John Hasler, Chamberlain to the Lord Lieutenant; Mr. William Macartney, father of Sir John Macartney, of Rochestown, who had represented Belfast in Parliament for many years; Mr. John Patrickson, and Miss Charlotte Brooke, authoress of "Reliques of Irish Poetry." There was then a scheme to build a crescent of houses, and to construct a bathing-place, as well as to make the present road from Kingstown to Dalkey, but building to any extent did not commence until some thirty years later, when speculators were attracted to Dalkey in hope of finding gold, and found wealth, not in ore, but in the value of the building sites[112].

DALKEY ISLAND.

THE ruined church, for such undoubtedly is the structure on the northern end of Dalkey Island, is coeval with and similar in construction to that of Kill-of-the-Grange. It has a primitive doorway and window, and its side walls

---

[112] Book of Postings and Sale; Gaskins' "Irish Varieties"; "Dictionary of National Biography," vol. vii., p. 224: Wilson's "Topographical Description of Dalkey," in *Exshaw's Magazine* for 1770, p. 485; Rutty's "Natural History of the County Dublin," vol. ii., p. 140; Cooper's Note Book; Newspaper Cuttings relating to Ireland in the British Museum; Ferrar's "View of Dublin," p. 77.

project beyond the end ones, as do those of Kill Church, forming pilasters. The belfry is a later addition; and a fireplace and enlarged doorway and window in the south wall were made by the workmen employed in the construction of the Martello Tower, who used it as their dwelling. Near the church there is a sacred well, and on one of the rocks a curious cross is engraved[113].

Dalkey Island and the Muglins in 1795.
From a Plate drawn by F. Jukes.

Before the Christian era, according to the Four Masters in the year of the world 3501, a dun, or fort, was erected, on Dalkey Island, by Sedgha, a Milesian chieftain, of great renown. During the Danish invasions the island was used as a place of refuge. Coibhdeanach, Abbot of Cillachoidh, was drowned near it in 938, while fleeing from the Norsemen; and the few Danes who escaped from Dublin, in 942, when it was destroyed by the Irish, fled to the island in ships. The church, which is supposed to have been dedicated to St. Beguet, the patron saint of Dalkey, who possibly retired from the worldly pleasures of the mainland to the island, indicates, by its state of preservation, use in the later middle ages; but nothing is recorded of the history of the island from the twelfth century, when it was given by Hugh de Lacy to the See of Dublin, until the seventeenth century, when it was destitute of inhabitants and used for grazing of cattle. In the succeeding century it saw some changing scenes, and was the subject of various projects. In 1738 it was selected by Lord and Lady Tullamore, then living at Dunleary, as the scene of an

---

[113] Wakeman's "Primitive Churches in the County Dublin," in the *Journal, R.S.A.I.,* vol. xxi., p. 701, also see vol. xxvi., p. 415.

entertainment, to celebrate the Battle of the Boyne, at which many loyal toasts were drunk. In 1766 it saw the bodies of two noted pirates hanging in an iron case on the adjacent Muglin rocks. And, towards the close of the century, it was made the object for boating excursions by the Viceroys while staying at Blackrock House, and was the scene of extraordinary revels, presided over by "His facetious Majesty, Stephen the First, King of Dalkey, Emperor of the Muglins, Prince of the Holy Island of Magee, Elector of Lambay and Ireland's Eye, Defender of his own faith and Respecter of all others, Sovereign of the illustrious Order of the Lobster and Periwinkle." It was suggested as the basis of a harbour and the site of a prison, and during the terror of French invasion, was guarded by some troops and a few small guns[114].

Ruined Church on Dalkey Island.
From a Photograph by Thomas Mason

---

[114] "Annals of the Four Masters," D'Alton's "History of the County Dublin," 887; Boate's "Natural History of Ireland;" *Dublin Evening Post,* July 1-4, 1738; Gaskins' "Irish Varieties"; "Ireland Sixty Years Ago," p. 139; *Dublin Journal,* No. 6847; *Dublin Chronicle,* 1787-1788, p. 928, 1788-1789, p. 143, 1791-1792, p. 1062.

West Doorway of the Ruined Church of Dalkey.
From a Photograph by J. P. O'Reilly.

Ruined Church of Dalkey.
From a Photograph by Eduard Bradford.

Ecclesiastical History.

ADJACENT to the castle, now incorporated in the Town Hall, stands the ruined church of Dalkey. The remains comprise a nave and chancel, and, although the church was evidently rebuilt, still include a primitive doorway and window. The most remarkable feature of the ruins, however, is the belfry on the western end, and a flight of steps, by which it is approached. It has openings for two bells, and it has been suggested, from the facility for access to them, that they were sounded by being struck and not by being tolled. In the graveyard, at least one stone with concentric markings, supposed by some to be of Pagan origin, has been discovered[115].

The church was dedicated to St. Beguet the Virgin the patron saint of Dalkey, who is supposed to have flourished about the seventh century, and whose festival falls on the 12th November. After the English Conquest it was assigned to the Priory of the Holy Trinity, but, as mentioned in the history of Kill-of-the-Grange, subsequently formed portion of the prebend of Clonkeen, in St. Patrick's Cathedral. It was restored to the Priory in the middle of the thirteenth century, and was, in 1324, one of the churches over which the Archdeacon of Dublin demanded a right of visitation. He cited "the discreet man, the Chaplain of Dalkey," to appear before him, and, on resistance being offered to him, pronounced sentence of excommunication on all concerned in the opposition. In the sixteenth century, on the dissolution of the Priory, the church was assigned to the Dean of the newly-founded Cathedral, and we find amongst its chaplains, in 1524, James White, Archdeacon of Armagh; in 1566, John Sheridan, and, in 1587, Morgan Byrne. They had also to serve the parish of Killiney, and were provided with a house and had a right of fishing. At the close of that century the tithes in consideration of assistance given in re-building the Cathedral spire, were leased by the Chapter to Richard Fagan, of Bullock. The opening of the

---

[115] "Ante-Norman Churches in the County Dublin," by W. F. Wakeman; and "Leacs and Crosses in the Half Barony of Rathdown," by P. J. O'Reilly, in *Journal R.S.A.I.*, vol. xxii., p. 103, and vol. xxxi., pp. 147-158, also see vol. xxvi., p. 411, and vol. xi., p. 209; "On the Mode of Ringing Bells in the early Churches of Spain and Ireland," by Joseph P. O'Reilly, in *Proceedings of the Royal Irish Academy*, 3rd Ser., vol. vi., p. 489.

seventeenth century found the church in a ruinous condition, and the only attendants at the services, excepting in the fishing season, when English and Scotch fishermen resorted to Dalkey, were the curate's family. Amongst those who held the cure, at a stipend of £4 a year, were, in 1615, the Rev. Owen Ellis, the curate of Kill-of-the-Grange; in 1630, the Rev. William Morris Lloyd, the curate of Monkstown; in 1640, the Rev. John Wilson, who was forced by the rebels to fly to Dublin, and there died from "want of relief in his sickness"; and, in 1642, the Rev. James Bishop, a Fellow of Trinity College, who was ordained that year. Bishop was the last of its curates. After the Restoration the parish was united to Monkstown, and the Church of St. Begnet has not since been used[116].

---

[116] Archdall's "Monasticon Hibernicum," edited by Archbishop Moran, vol. i. p. 2; "Obits and Martyrology of Christ Church," p. xlv.; Christ Church Deeds; "Chartularies of St. Mary's Abbey," vol. i., p. 528; Archbishop Bulkeley's Report; Depositions of 1641; Diocesan Records.

PARISH OF KILLINEY.

The Parish of Killiney is shown on the Down Survey Maps of 1657, as consisting of the Townlands of Killeney, Hackettsland, and Loughnanstowne.

Killeney is now represented by the Townland of Killiney; Hackettsland is represented by Hackettsland; Loughnanstowne is represented by Loughlinstown (*i.e.* Baile-an-Lochain, the town of the little lake), Ballybrack (*i.e.* speckled town), part of Kilbogget, and Cherrywood.

There are the following objects of archæological interest in the parish—Cromlech near Shanganagh, "Druid's Judgment Seat" at Killiney, and ruined Church of Killiney.

KILLINEY.

Cromlech near Ballybrack in 1777.
From a Drawing by Gabriel Beranger.

"Druid's Judgment Seat"
From a Photograph in the Collection of the Royal Society of Antiquaries of Ireland.

TWO monuments of the primeval age are to be found on the lands of Killiney. One of these is a Cromlech, which stands near the road leading from Ballybrack to Shanganagh. It is, as compared with others in the County Dublin, a small specimen, and, owing to some of the supporting stones being broken, the roof rock, which weighs about twelve tons, has fallen somewhat from its original position[117]. The other monument of the rock age is near the Martello Tower, at Killiney, and is known as "the Druids' judgment seat." In its present form it is a modern antique, but the stones of which it is composed formed part of a sepulchral memorial, dating from very early times. The latter consisted of three small Cromlechs, surrounded by a circle of upright stones, about 135 feet in circumference, and, at the time of its first attracting attention, in the eighteenth century, when everything pre-historic was attributed either to the Druids or the Danes, it was assumed to be a Pagan

---

[117] "The Rock Monuments of the County Dublin," by Henry O'Neill, *Journal R.S.A.I.*, vol. ii. p. 41; Borlase's "Dolmens of Ireland," vol. ii., p. 392.

temple—a designation under which it is marked on the Ordnance Survey Map. Near the circle was discovered at the same time an ancient burying-place, and some stones with curious markings, which are still to be seen. The burying-place was of considerable extent, the bodies, which were enclosed in coffins made of flags, having been laid in a number of rows of ten each[118].

Before the English invasion the lands of Killiney had been given to the Priory of the Holy Trinity, and subsequently they were confirmed to it, with those of Kill-of-the-Grange, by the ecclesiastical and lay authorities. They were included in the Manor of Kill-of-the-Grange, and, in spite of their rocky and sterile character, they were inhabited, in the fourteenth century, by John Milis, and many cottagers, who were bound to do "divers' works" on the home farm of the Priory, and who contributed fifteen reapers at harvest time. After the dissolution of the Priory the lands were held successively, under the Cathedral, by William Walsh, *alias* McHowell; James Garvey, doubtless a relative of the Primate of that name, who had been Dean of Christ Church; and the owners of Loughlinstown, the Goodman family. After the Rebellion of 1641, the property of the Goodmans was confiscated and seized by the Parliament. On the Restoration the lands of Killiney were recovered for the Cathedral by Dr. Lightburne, and were afterwards held by Gilbert Wye, of Belfast, an officer in the Earl of Donegal's regiment, the Mossoms, already mentioned as owners of Tipperstown, the Fawcetts, who were owners of Brenanstown, and the Pocklingtons and Domviles, of whom we shall see under Loughlinstown. Towards the close of the eighteenth century, "a neat lodge" was built near the ruined church by Mr. Peter Wilson, who removed there from Dalkey, on retiring from business, and it was in his grounds, in 1785, that the stone remains and burying-place, which, on his invitation, were inspected by General Vallancey, were discovered. Later on a Mr. Fetherston was residing at Killiney, and, in 1800, the Rev. James Dunn then curate, and afterwards vicar, of Monkstown, was lodging in "a small cottage, delightfully situated over the seashore." In the year 1788—a remarkable one in the annals of Killiney—a coal brig, which had gone ashore on the strand, and whose recovery had been given up as hopeless by English engineers, was floated by a Dublin firm; and a prodigious boy, who at seven years of age was 5 feet 2

---

[118] *Dublin Chronicle,* 1787-1788, pp. 464, 492, 520; *Dublin Penny Journal,* vol. ii., p. 256; *Journal R.S.A. I.,* vol. xxvi., p. 411.

inches high and 4 feet 5 inches round his waist, was to be seen at Ballybrack[119]. During the first part of the nineteenth century Killiney was still open country, as the fatal accident, in 1815, to the Duke of Dorset—the stepson of Lord Whitworth, the Viceroy of the time—while hunting on its lands, indicates[120] but its beauty later on became more appreciated, and a great speculative building scheme, with "views perspective as well as prospective," of which Victoria Castle was the outcome, was laid before the public[121].

LOUGHLINSTOWN.

A PORTION of Loughlinstown House, the residence of Major Herbert W. Domvile, D.L., at present High Sheriff of the County Dublin, dates from the Restoration period of the seventeenth century. The front of the house, which is approached by a winding drive of modern construction, is a comparatively recent erection, but the back, which forms three sides of a square, and which was approached more directly from the road by an avenue now disused, is evidently a much older structure.

The lands of Loughlinstown, which, as their name and formation indicate, formerly contained a small lake, belonged, in the middle ages, to the Talbots, the owners of Rochestown, and were held under them by the Goodmans, who were also early English settlers. The Goodmans were, doubtless, originally placed there as hardy warders of the Pale—men capable of guarding its barrier, which ran not far off, and of offering effective resistance to the incursions of the Irish tribes; but in the sixteenth century they had become men of note, and filled the offices of Sheriff and of Commissioner for the Muster of the Militia. As cattle afforded too tempting plunder to the marauders, the lands were devoted to tillage and, in addition to a castle for themselves, the Goodmans erected a large and strong barn for the storage of their corn, which

---

[119] Christ Church Deeds; "Account Roll of the Priory of the Holy Trinity"; Cooper's Note Book; *Dublin Chronicle*, 1788-1789, pp. 128, 294; Diary of Alexander Hamilton, LL.D., K.C.; Sleater's "Topography of Ireland."

[120] A monument on the hill bears the following inscription, "This pile was raised to mark the fatal spot where, at the age of 21, George John Frederick, the fourth Duke of Dorset, accidentally lost his life 14th February, 1815." See Plumptre's "Residence in Ireland," p. 84.

[121] *Irish Penny Journal*, vol. i., p. 385

was ground in a mill upon the river. In the first half of the sixteenth century, Loughlinstown was held by James Goodman, who, in 1547, was given a grant of land in the County Wicklow, which the Government then desired to colonise, and he was succeeded by his son, of the same name, already mentioned as tenant of the lands of Rochestown and Cornelscourt. The latter, whom we find in the same year rescuing a prisoner from the sub-sheriff, and given a commission to execute martial law, held also the lands of Danestown, at Castleknock, and, as a large tillage farmer and loyal subject, agreed, in 1572, to supply the garrison with corn, at a price to be fixed by the Council, and to forgive the Crown all money due to him for provisioning the army from "the beginning of the world" to that time.

After his death, in 1575, when, notwithstanding his being a Roman Catholic, he was buried, as were all his family, in the parish church of Killiney, Loughlinstown passed successively to his son, Richard, who died in 1589; to his son, William, who signed the assurance of loyalty from the Roman Catholics of the Pale, on the accession of James I., and who died in 1622; and to his grandson, James, whose father, Gilbert, had died in 1615. James Goodman was in possession of the lands when the Rebellion of 1641 broke out, and the English Government found in him a most active and determined enemy. In all the depositions made by his neighbours, he is mentioned as foremost in deeds of cruelty and rapine, and he was guilty of at least one murder, for which, under the Commonwealth, he was executed. His victim was a tenant of his own, called William Boatson, and the murder was committed in cold blood in a camp which the rebels had at Bray. On the rebel stronghold at Carrickmines being taken in the following March, a company of a regiment, commanded by the well-known General Monk, who was created, after the Restoration, Duke of Albemarle, was stationed at Loughlinstown, and Goodman, who served subsequently as Provost-Marshal in the army of the Confederates, was forced to flee[122].

---

[122] Fiants, Edward VI. and Elizabeth; Calendar of State Papers, Ireland, 1509-1573, p. 62, 1603-1606, p. 363; Calendar of Carew State Papers, 1515-1574, p. 419, 1589-1600, p. 188; Exchequer Inquisition, Co. Dublin, Elizabeth, No. 204, Jac. I. No. 77; "Description of Ireland in 1598," edited by Rev. Edmund Hogan, p. 37; Archbishop Bulkeley's Report; Historical Manuscripts Commission, Rept. 14, App., pt. vii., vol. i., p. 136; Hickson's "Ireland in the Seventeenth Century," vol. i. p. 232; Depositions of 1641.

Loughlinstown in 1820.
From a Plate drawn by George Petrie in Cromwell's "Excursions through Ireland."

Loughlinstown then became forfeited property, and was set forth in the surveys, made by direction of the Parliament, as a most desirable estate, with "a fair pleasant river" running through it, and with a substantial residence and offices, surrounded by a garden and orchard, in good repair. It was subsequently designated, in addition to Monkstown, for Edmund Ludlow, but, as his sister wrote to him, one had "to labour for resigned hearts" in those changing times, and "the rich mercy" of its settlement on him, for which she prayed, was not vouchsafed. During the Commonwealth a colony of its adherents settled in the neighbourhood, and had at times the advantage of the ministrations of the Provost of Trinity College, Dr. Samuel Winter, an active opponent of the doctrine of the Anabaptists, who records the names of several children baptised by him at Loughlinstown. On its lands there were then eight inhabitants of English and sixty-eight of Irish extraction, of whom the principal was Mr. John Lambert, who occupied Goodman's house, and who was subsequently evicted[123].

With the Restoration, the Domvile family came to Loughlinstown, in the person of Sir William Domvile, Attorney-General for Ireland during the reign of Charles II., who was granted the lands by his Royal master, and whose descendants have held them uninterruptedly to the present time. Domvile, owing to his great ability, occupied a prominent position in the Ireland of his day, and his family has ever since taken a first place in the metropolitan county. He was descended from an ancient Cheshire family, and was the eldest son of Gilbert Domvile, an Irish legal official, who married a daughter of Dr. Thomas Jones, Archbishop of Dublin, and Chancellor of Ireland, and became M.P. for the borough of Donegal. After completing his education at Oxford, Domvile was called to the English Bar, where he continued to practise until the Restoration, and where he displayed such legal attainments as resulted in his election as a Bencher of his Inn. While a student he married a daughter of Sir Thomas Lake, one of the Secretaries of State of James I., and, though for a time the eccentricities of Lady Lake, who had brought about her husband's ruin, caused him annoyance, the alliance resulted in much happiness. Through his wife Domvile had made many influential connections

---

[123] Fleetwood's Survey; Down Survey; "Ludlow's Memoirs," edited by C. H. Firth, vol. ii., p. 444; Census of 1659; Hearth Money Roll; Provost Winter's Papers preserved in Trinity College Library.

amongst the Royalists, and his own family, both on the side of the Domviles and of the Joneses, elevated under the title of Ranelagh to the peerage, had shown unswerving devotion to the throne. To his interest, combined with his learning as a lawyer, his appointment on the Restoration as "the King's Attorney" in Ireland was due, and his conduct during the twenty-six years he occupied that office showed that his promotion was deserved.

Sir William Domvile, Knight.
From a Portrait in the possession of Major H. W. Domvile.

Before he left London Domvile received from the King the honour of knighthood, and on his arrival in this country, was elected Knight of the Shire for the County Dublin. The Government were desirous that he should be elected Speaker of the House of Commons, but his sympathies were known to lie on the side of the early English settlers, and the interest of their opponents, the adventurers, and the soldiers, was too strong in the House to permit of his candidature being pressed with success. The business of the settlement fell to his office, and Domvile, although he tried to steer an even course, incurred in its discharge much public obloquy, and failed to please either party—the later settlers speaking of him as an enemy to their interests, and the early settlers as indifferent and lukewarm to their claims. His services in that arduous work, and as Chief Prosecutor, were however, fully recognised by the Crown, and so great were the emoluments and perquisites of his office that on two occasions he refused the Chief Justiceship of the Court of Common Pleas, stating that if his promotion were pressed he would consider it a mark of disfavour.

On the lands of Loughlinstown Domvile erected, in place of the mediæval castle, a modern house, where he delighted to retire from the cares of business. The house was not a large one, and can have afforded little accommodation beyond the principal rooms—the hall, the great parlour, and the little parlour, and the great bedchamber, which were hung, after the manner of the time, with tapestry hangings and embroidered curtains. The accommodation was sufficient, however, to allow Domvile to indulge his wide literary tastes, and to enjoy the companionship of his children, whose welfare was ever his main object. At Loughlinstown also he amused himself, with the help of faithful and attached retainers who found in him the best of masters, in breeding black cattle, and sheep, and saddle coach, and draught horses, of which his draught nag, "Scully Bote," and his grey nag, "Fisher," had first place in his affections.

Domvile, who had been removed from the Attorney-Generalship not long after the accession of James II., died in 1689, while Ireland was in the turmoil caused by that monarch's occupation. Loughlinstown passed then to his eldest son, who bore the same name as himself, and who had been knighted by the Duke of Ormonde—a staunch friend of his father's—before his resignation of the sword. Sir William Domvile, the second, had represented the Borough of Antrim in Parliament during his father's lifetime, but owing to ill-health he did not subsequently take any part in public affairs. During his ownership of Loughlinstown, James II., and his army, according to tradition, encamped there, and an ancient tree near the house is said to have been planted by James with his own hands. After this Sir William's death, which took place in 1698, Loughlinstown came into the possession of his eldest son, another William Domvile, who was pronounced by Swift "to be perfectly as fine a gentleman as he knew." With the exception of a few years, during which he was elected, in 1717, as Knight of the Shire for the County Dublin, he was a permanent absentee from Ireland, spending his time in London and abroad, where be cultivated literary society and lived the life of a man of fashion. During his time Loughlinstown House was uninhabited, and Mrs. Delaney, who observed that it was ingeniously situated to avoid one of the sweetest prospects imaginable, speaks of it, in 1752, as old and ruinous[124].

Loughlinstown was then the centre of the Kilruddery hunt district, and was best known as the site of an inn the favourite resort of hunting-men, which stood opposite the gate of Loughlinstown House, and is now converted into a villa, called Beechgrove. There the sound of the cheery horn was often to be heard, and the hunt in full cry to be seen. The inn was kept by the sporting landlord, the bold Owen Bray, whose exploits on his blind horse have been commemorated by the actor, Thomas Mozeen, in his lines on the Kilruddery Hunt, and right royally did he entertain his guests. In "An Invitation to Owen Bray's," Mozeen, who often was one of them, advises all travellers sick of the seas to repair there, and to drain to the eighty-fourth bumper the quick moving bottles of Bray's famous claret. Bray did not confine his trade to that of an innkeeper, but was ever willing to send to his

---

[124] 15th Report of Record Commissioners; Burke's "Peerage and Baronetage"; under Domvile and Domville; Ormerod's "History of Cheshire"; Calendar of State Papers, Ireland, 1611-1614, p. 442, 1625-1632, pp. 23, 412; Foster's "Alumni Oxonienses"; "Calendar of Domestic State Papers," 1636-1637, p. 192, 1623-1625, p. 430; Lincoln's Inn Admissions and Black Book; Smyth's "Law Officers of Ireland"; "State Letters of the Earl of Orrery," vol. i., p. 34; Carte Papers; "Papers of the Earl of Dartmouth," published by Historical Manuscripts Commission; Letter Book and Correspondence of the Earl of Essex in British Museum, Stowe MSS.; Wills of the Domviles; "Correspondence of Henry Hyde, Earl of Clarendon, and of Laurence Hyde, Earl of Rochester," edited by S. W. Singer; Ferrar's "View of Dublin," p. 124; Prior's "List of the Absentees of Ireland"; Scott's "Works of Swift," vols. ii. and iii.; "Letters of Mary Lepel, Lady Hervey," pp. 257, 261; "Life and Correspondence of Mary Granville, Mrs. Delany," vol. iii., pp. 120, 125.

neighbours' houses joints of venison and mutton, and bottles of claret and Lisbon, and even a loan of money when necessary[125].

Sir Thomas Domvile, Bart.
From a Portrait in the possession of Major H. W. Domvile.

On Mr. Domvile's death, which occurred in 1763, his property passed to his cousin, Sir Compton Domvile, the only son of the Attorney-General's second son Thomas, who had been created a baronet. Sir Compton, who was a Privy Councillor, represented the County Dublin in Parliament for many years, and held the Clerkship of the Crown and Hanaper, which had been in the family from the Attorney-General's time. In addition to his seat at Templeogue, which had belonged to his father, he had succeeded to Santry Court, on the death of his nephew, the last Lord Santry, and, as a residence, he made no use of Loughlinstown House. His death took place five years later, in 1768, and as he died without issue, he left his property to his nephew, Charles Pocklington, his second sister's son by her marriage to Admiral

---

[125] O'Keeffe's "Recollections of his Life." vol. i., p. 23 *Notes and Queries,* 3rd Ser. v., 500-504; Mozeen's "Collection of Miscellaneous Essays," p. 59.

Christopher Pocklington. Loughlinstown, however, had been entailed by Mr. William Domvile, and, on Sir Compton's death, went to Mr. Domvile's own nephew, the Rev. Benjamin Barrington, who took as did Pocklington, the name of Domvile. Dr. Barrington was Dean of Armagh at the time of his succession to Loughlinstown, but he came then to Dublin, exchanged that dignity for Dublin preferment, and though well advanced in life, took unto himself a wife in the person of his cousin, a sister of Charles Pocklington. He first held the vicarage of St. Ann's, in Dublin, but shortly before his death, in 1774, he was appointed to the rectory of Bray and prebend of Rathmichael[126].

Sir Compton Domvile, Bart.
From a Portrait in the possession of Major H. W. Domvile.

Dr. Barrington Domvile, who was distinguished for his charitable disposition, and had a high reputation as a preacher[127], did not reside at

---

[126] *Freeman's Journal*, vol. v., No. 57, Sept. 26, 1884; *Exshaw's Magazine*, 1768, p.256.

[127] A mural tablet in Monkstown Church bears the following inscription, "Sacred to the memory of Benjamin Domvile, D.D., who was born May 19th, 1711, and died October 18th, 1774. He entertained the deepest sense of the importance, and exerted the most conscientious

Loughlinstown, but after his death the house was enlarged, and the grounds newly laid out by a nephew of his wife's, Mr. Francis Savage—a young man of much promise as an eloquent speaker—and subsequently the house became the residence of Mrs. Barrington Domvile[128]. During the last century, until of very recent years, it has been let by the owners, and, for the greater half of that century, it was the residence of the Honourable Robert Day, one of the judges of the King's Bench, who was in early life one of Grattan's most intimate friends, and who has been described as an eloquent advocate, an able lawyer, and a just and merciful judge[129].

HACKETTSLAND.

THESE lands, doubtless, derive their name from the Hackets, who were, in the fourteenth century, one of the principal families in the southern part of the County Dublin, and, probably, in 1344, Thomas Hacket, whose servingman was employed by the Priory of the Holy Trinity to watch the tithes of Killiney and Loughlinstown, was the owner. In the seventeenth century the lands were owned by the Wolverstons, of Stillorgan, and, in the following century, a family called Towson was resident on them[130].

---

diligence, in the discharge of his sacred office his discourses, addressed to the understanding and the heart, were so powerfully enforced by animated language and strength of reasoning, that he was justly admired as the most persuasive preacher of his time. Equally respected in private life his filial piety, conjugal affection, and tender regard to all his family, were most exemplary. Invariable in friendship, unbounded in benevolence, the great object of his constant endeavours was to promote the honour of God and the happiness of mankind. This humble monument was erected by his grateful and afflicted widow."

[128] *Exshaw's Magazine,* 1785, p. 614; Coopers Note Book; Lewis' "Dublin Guide."

[129] The following inscription appears on a mural tablet in Monkstown Church, "Sacred to the memory of Robert Day, Esquire, late second Justice of the Court of King's Bench in Ireland. He was third son of the Rev. John Day, of Lohercannon, in the County of Kerry, and of Lucy, his wife, daughter of Maurice Fitz-Gerald, Knight of Kerry. He died 8th February, 1841, in the 85th year of his age. He was an eloquent advocate, an able lawyer, and a just and merciful judge. His affectionate widow erected this monument as a slight tribute to his many virtues, and in the hope of his resurrection to eternal life, through our Lord Jesus Christ." He was buried in Monkstown graveyard, where there is a tombstone to his memory.

[130] "Account Roll of the Priory of the Holy Trinity;" Fleetwood's Survey: Certificates of Innocents, iv., 17; Grand Jury Panel; *Exshaw's Magazine,* 1755, p. 104.

Kilbogget.

THE tithes of these lands, part of which formerly lay within the parish of Kill-of-the-Grange, and on which a primitive church stood, belonged to the Priory of the Holy Trinity, and, at the close of the sixteenth century, were leased by the Cathedral of Christ Church to Alderman Gerald Young, of Dublin. The lands were then owned by the Rochfort family, who were subsequently dispossessed for the part which they took in the Rebellion, and, after the Restoration, the lands were granted to Sir William Domvile, together with those of Loughlinstown[131].

Ecclesiastical History.

THE ruined church of Killiney has been pronounced by Dr. Petrie to be coeval with the oldest of the buildings at Glendalough, and to date from the sixth century. The original structure consisted of the nave and chancel, and to these were added, many centuries later, an aisle on the northern side. The primitive doorway in the western end, which bears on the soffit of its lintel a cross, the choir arch, and the east window are all very characteristic of early Irish church architecture[132].

The name of Cill-inghen-Leinin, the early form of Killiney, indicates that the church was founded by Leinin's daughters, five holy women, whose names, according to the Martyrology of Donegal, were, Druigen, Luigen, Luicell, Macha, and Riomhtach, and who are supposed to have flourished about the sixth century. Together with the lands, the church came into the possession of the Priory of the Holy Trinity before the English Conquest, and was subsequently confirmed to it by the Archbishop of Dublin and the Pope. After the dissolution of the Priory it became portion of the dignity of the Dean of Christ Church, and appears to have been served, in the sixteenth

---

[131] Christ Church Deeds; Fleetwood's Survey; Certificates for Adventurers and Soldiers, iii.,179.

[132] Petrie's "Essay on the Round Towers," p. 170; Ante-Norman Churches in the County Dublin," by W. F. Wakeman, *Journal, R.S.A.I.,* vol. xxii., p. 101 *Irish Literary Gazette,* vol. i., p. 169.

century, by the chaplains of Dalkey. At the beginning of the seventeenth century, in 1615, it was in charge of the vicar of Bray, the Rev. Morris Burne, but was subsequently held by the same curates as Dalkey—the Rev. William Morris Lloyd, the Rev. John Wilson, and the Rev. James Bishop. The tithes which the Dean enjoyed amounted to £24, and the curate's stipend was only £6 per annum. The church was then roofless, as it has since remained, and there was not a Protestant in the parish. The Roman Catholics, who, at the close of the preceding century, had made an effort to build themselves a chapel, had service constantly performed in the house of the owner of Loughlinstown, and had a school for their children, in which they were taught by one of their faith[133].

Ruined Church of Killiney.
From a Photograph by Thomas Mason.

---

[133] O'Hanlon's "Lives of the Irish Saints," vol. iii., 1. 196; Christ Church Deeds; Exchequer Inquisition, County Dublin, Eliz., No. 204; Regal Visitation of 1615; Archbishop Bulkeley's Report.

At the beginning of the eighteenth century there was a parish priest of Killiney, the Rev. William Dardis, who lived at Kill-of-the-Grange. Towards the close of that century, owing to the lethargic condition of the Established Church, the Methodists held revival meetings in the neighbourhood, and, in 1782, the Rev. Edward Smyth, one of their clergymen, came to reside at Killiney, and there was, his wife writes, "a noise and a shaking among the dry bones."[134]

---

[134] "Return of Roman Catholic Clergy in 1704"; Crookshank's "History of Methodism in Ireland," vol. i., p. 360.

PARISH OF TULLY.

(Formerly called Tolach na n-Escop, the Hill of the Bishops).

This parish is shown on the Down Survey Map, made in 1657, as consisting of the townlands of Loughenstowne, Brenanstowne, Carrickmaine and Glanamuok, and Leperstowne.

Loughenstowne is now represented by the townland of Laughanstown, and included apparently the Glebe of Rathmichael.

Brenanstowne is represented by Brenanstown.

Carrickmaine and Glanamuck is represented by Carrickmines (*i.e.,* Carraigmaighin, the Little Plain of Rocks) Great, Tiknick Tigh (*i.e.,* Cnuic, the House on the Hill), Kingston, Glenamuck (*i.e.,* Glean na muc, the valley of the pigs) North and South, Jamestown, Ballyogan, Carrickmines Little, and Kerrymount.

Leperstowne is represented by Leopardstown and Carmanhall.

The townlands of Murphystown and Blackthorn, now included in Tully Parish, are shown on the Down Survey as in Taney parish, under the name of Moltanstowne.

The parish contains the following objects of archæological interest:— Cromlech, near Brenanstown; ruined Church of Tully, and remains of Castles of Carrickmines and Murphystown.

CARRICKMINES CASTLE.

A FRAGMENT of an ancient building, new forming the end wall of a piggery, is to be found in a farmyard not far from the railway station of Carrickmines, on the right-hand side of the road leading to Golden Ball. It is of massive proportions, and contains a light or window[135].

---

[135] Joyce's "Rambles in the County Dublin," p. 49, in *Evening Telegraph Reprints;* Cooper's Note Book.

This fragment is all that remains of a strongly-fortified castle, which was erected at Carrickmines, after the English Conquest, to protect the south marches of the City of Dublin. These, owing to Carrickmines being the most convenient route for the Irish tribes in making their raids, were exposed at that point to much danger, and by the aid of the castle the marauders were often successfully opposed before they descended on the cultivated lands of Kill-of-the-Grange and Monkstown. The castle was garrisoned by a branch of the Walsh family, to which the lands of Carrickmines, or the Little Plain of Rocks, had been given, and its occupants combined in a remarkable degree the aptitude for martial and for agricultural pursuits necessary to make them successful colonists. At first they were not able to withstand alone the attacks of the enemy from the mountains, and, in the fourteenth century, troops were despatched from time to time to their assistance. Thus there were stationed at Carrickmines, in 1360, a troop of light horsemen, under the leadership of Sir John Bermingham; in 1375, a large force, under the command of a famous ecclesiastic, John Colton, then Dean of St. Patrick's and Treasurer of Ireland, and after wards Archbishop of Armagh, who stayed at Carrickmines on one occasion for three days, and on another for a month; and, in 1388, forty mounted archers, for whose support a contribution was levied from the distant lands of Fingal.

But, in the beginning of the fifteenth century, the Walshes had established a reputation for prowess in the field which kept the tribes in more awe, and allowed the Walshes to devote more attention to the cultivation of their lands. Henry Walsh, who was then their captain, was, in 1441, allowed by the Crown ten marks—a large sum in those days—for protecting the liegemen, and probably it was by him that the Castle of Carrickmines was erected in the form in which it stood for the next two centuries. The lands of Carrickmines, which were held direct from the Crown by military service, had been conveyed to his grandfather, Henry, son of Adam Walsh, by John and David Walsh, and had come subsequently into the possession of his father, William Walsh, who, in 1407, was residing on part of them called Symondstown. Henry Walsh had succeeded to the lands in 1420, and, as he was then a minor, portion of his property was committed to an ecclesiastic, Richard Northorp, by name, who was exempted from rendering any account with respect to it during the minority[136].

The sixteenth century found the Walshes in occupation, either as tenants or owners, of a very wide extent of country, and they had become one of the most important families on the southern side of Dublin. The owners of the lands of Carrickmines, on which there was near the castle a hamlet called Ballinrow, and a water mill (whose site is marked on the Ordnance map), held also the lands of Kilpool and Old Court, in the County Wicklow, and were generally named amongst the officers responsible for the muster of the militia. Henry Walsh had died in 1481, and amongst his successors in the occupation of the castle we find Edmund Walsh, who, in 1519, was involved in litigation with the Priory of the Holy Trinity as to adjacent lands; William, son of Theobald Walsh, who married a daughter of the house of Fitzwilliam, and died in 1572; Richard, son of William Walsh, who married one of the Eustaces, and died in 1580; Theobald, son of Richard Walsh, who died in 1593; and Richard, son, of Theobald Walsh. Richard Walsh was a minor at the time of his father's death, and while his property was in the custody of Peter Barnewall, his guardian, the lands of Carrickmines were completely devastated by Irish marauders, who carried off "the prey of the town," notwithstanding the presence of a troop of horse, which was then stationed there[137].

At the beginning of the seventeenth century, the Walshes were described as a large and ancient stock, and as men of note in the metropolitan county, which was then "rich and plenteous in corn and cattle, and inhabited by a people of stately port and garb." The Castle of Carrickmines was surrounded by an orchard and garden, and, so far as was possible, its lands had been subjected to the plough[138]. But before the middle of that century the Walshes' prosperity was at an end, and they were reduced to the position of wanderers

---

[136] Patent and Close Rolls, pp. 79, 87, 136, 154, 216, 249, 263; "Dictionary of National Biography," vol. xi., p. 508; Records of Rolls in Public Record Office; "Chartularies of St. Mary's Abbey," vol, i., pp. 279-280, 531.

[137] Christ Church Deeds, Nos. 408, 1134; Fiants; Exchequer Inquisitions, Co. Dublin, Elizabeth, Nos. 139, 223; Calendar of State Papers, Ireland, 1599-1600. p. 63.

[138] "A Geographical Description of the Kingdom of Ireland," Lon. 1642, preserved in the Royal Irish Academy; "Description of Ireland in 1598" by the Rev. Edmund Hogan, p. 37.

on the earth. The part taken by the owner of Carrickmines, in the Rebellion of 1641, is not clear, but as a family the Walshes threw themselves with ardour on the Irish side, and proved that they had become at least as Irish as the Irish themselves. Whether with or without the consent of the owner, Carrickmines became the centre of disaffection in the southern part of the County Dublin, and the Walshes figure prominently in the depositions made by those who suffered losses during that dreadful winter. Richard Walsh, who had succeeded, in 1593, to Carrickmines, is stated in an inquisition to have died in 1620, but, according to the pedigree of a noble Austrian family, the Counts von Wallis, who claim descent from his second son, he did not die until some years later. His eldest son, Theobald, was, however, living, in 1630, in Carrickmines Castle. A payment was then made to him, on the order of a foreigner, by the Earl of Cork, and, in a report on the diocese of Dublin it is mentioned that he was maintaining at that time in the castle a priest and a friar, "to celebrate Mass and execute their functions." But he cannot have been in it when its overthrow came, as he survived the Rebellion, and acted as a captain in the Confederates' army[139].

During the whole winter after the Rebellion the County Dublin, south of the city, was in the hands of the rebels. Their defeat in February, 1642, at Dean's Grange, gave them, no doubt, a check, and they fell back upon Carrickmines Castle, which they had prepared to stand a siege. Although the cannon, which had been brought from Bullock, appears to have been soon sent back, the castle was not left without arms, and, as events proved, was capable of affording very effective resistance. In it the main body of the rebels were assembled on a Saturday morning, at the end of March, when scouts came running in to tell them that troops were approaching, and before long they saw some horse drawing near. The horse were few in number and the rebels treated them with scorn and contempt. But the rebels did not take into account that the troops were commanded by one of the best officers in the English army, Sir Simon Harcourt, an ancestor of the well-known statesman of the present day, Sir William Vernon Harcourt, who had just returned from Munster, where he had displayed extraordinary energy in reducing the

---

[139] D'Alton's "King James' Irish Army List," 2nd ed., vol. ii., p. 212; Fleetwoods' Survey; Down Survey; "Pedigree of the Walshes," by Valentine Hussey Walsh, in *The Genealogist,* vol. xvii, pp. 217-224; "The Lismore Papers," Series i., vol. iii., p. 43; Archbishop Bulkeley's Report.

country to obedience. Harcourt's high spirit could ill bear the insolent demeanour of the defenders, but he was a prudent officer, and saw from the great strength of the castle that he could not successfully assail it with his small force. He, therefore, restrained himself until reinforcements arrived, to the number of 800 foot and sufficient horse to complete a troop of 250, and as it was then too late to commence operations, he placed a cordon round the castle, and guarded it all night.

During the darkness the defenders lighted a fire on the roof of the castle, which was answered by others from the hills, and Harcourt becoming alarmed, sent in to the authorities for further assistance. Meantime, the defenders made a vigorous attempt to break through the cordon, and kept up a brisk musket fire from the castle. By means of it they inflicted loss on the besiegers and terminated the gallant Harcourt's career. He had sought cover behind a small cottage, but stood up for a moment to issue some command to the soldiers, and, on being perceived by one of the defenders, who had already done great execution amongst the besiegers, was shot through the breast. He was carried off the field alive, but died next day at Lord Fitzwilliam's Castle, at Merrion. An additional 400 men had arrived, with two cannon, and Lieutenant-Colonel Gibson, who now took command, ordered a vigorous bombardment of the castle. The troops were roused to redoubled vigour by the loss of Harcourt, who was much beloved, and when an entry into the castle was secured, they rushed in, headed by Lieutenant Robert Hammond, afterwards famous as Governor of Carisbrooke Castle during the detention of Charles I. in the Isle of Wight, and fell upon the defenders with great fury. Fearful slaughter ensued on that Sunday evening in the peaceful valley of Carrickmines. All who were in the castle, men, women, and children, estimated to be 300 persons, were put to the sword, and the castle was blown up and levelled with the ground. The loss of the besiegers is said to have been only seven killed and nine wounded, but it included, besides Harcourt, one officer, Lieutenant Richard Cooke, killed, and another, Sergeant-Major Berry, mortally wounded. The resistance offered by the defenders to what was the flower of the English army in Ireland is very remarkable; but a statement made in the Aphorismical Discovery, that the castle was surrendered and not taken, does not appear to be well founded[140].

---

[140] "The Last True Intelligence from Ireland," Lon. 1642, preserved in the Royal Irish Academy; Borlase's "History of the Irish Rebellion," Lon. 1680, pp. 72-73; Clarendon's

After the Restoration the property of the Walshes, at Carrickmines, was awarded by the Commissioners of Settlement to the Earl of Meath, and was subsequently assigned by him to Sir Joshua Allen, of Stillorgan, whose representative, the Earl of Carysfort, is now lord of the soil. The population during the Commonwealth was returned as five English and fifty-four Irish, and five substantial houses and twenty-one cottages were erected on the lands. The adjoining lands of Glenamuck, which belonged also to the Walshes, and had been assigned to one Roger Jones, were wholly inhabited by Irish. In the middle of the eighteenth century the principal inhabitants of Carrickmines were Mr. Christopher Smalley and Mr. John Gravel. It was then acquiring a reputation as a health resort and, in the succeeding years, was much frequented by persons affected with pulmonary complaints, for whose accommodation lodgings were provided. Whey made from goats' milk was then the remedy recommended for consumption and kindred diseases; and the Dublin physicians, who, in the early part of the eighteenth century, sent their patients to the mountains of Mourne for the purpose of drinking it, found that, in addition to being more accessible, Carrickmines, where goats abounded, had an equally dry soil and more southern aspect. Many deaths are announced in the obituary columns of the newspapers of that day as taking place at Carrickmines, including, in 1760, the wife of Anthony Robinson, the Revenue Officer of Bullock, and a daughter of Thomas Morgan, sometime Recorder of Dublin; in 1761, John Payne, "an eminent livery lace weaver" in 1762, a daughter of Alderman Crampton; in 1772 George Carey, of Redcastle, "a gentleman of unbounded charity" in 1773, the Rev. Henry Wright, formerly curate of Monkstown; and, in 1780, Samuel Murphy, Doctor of Music, and a vicar-choral of St. Patrick's and Christ Church Cathedrals, names which indicate the universal belief at that time in the virtues of the air and treatment[141].

"History of the Rebellion and Civil War in Ireland," Lon. 1720, p. 245; "Dictionary of National Biography," vol. xxiv., pp. 248, 321; "Ormonde Papers," vol. i., p. 131, published by Historical Manuscripts Commissioners; "A Contemporary History of Affairs in Ireland from 1641 to 1652" edited by Sir John Gilbert, vol. i., p. 24.

[141] Certificates for Adventurers and Soldiers, vii., 166, 440; Census of 1659; Hearth Money Roll; Rutty's "Natural History of the County Dublin," vol. i., p. 272; *Dublin Journal*, No. 2605; *Pue's Occurrences,* vol. liv., No. 18, lvii., Nos. 27,62, lviii., No. 43, lix., No. 48; *Dublin Gazette,* Nos. 2497, 2627; *Exshaw's Magazine* for 1780, p. 632.

LAUGHANSTOWN

THESE lands which lie between Carrickmines and Loughlinstown, were originally known under the denomination of Tully, and were given, before the English Conquest, by Sigrahre, son of Thorkil, to the Priory of the Holy Trinity. Amongst their occupants from the fourteenth to the seventeenth century, we find the family of Macnebury, of Ashpoll, or Archbold, whose members were suspected of complicity in the murder of the owner of Bullock, and took part in the attack on that place, and of Crehall, in whose time a lease of the lands was given, probably for some legal purpose, to Thomas Smith, a Fellow of Trinity College. After the Restoration the lands, which had been seized by the Parliament, and leased to Dame Sara Reynolds, were recovered, with those of Killiney, by Dr. Lightburne, and were subsequently held by the same lessees. There was at the time of the Restoration on the lands a good thatched castle, which was occupied by Edward Buller, whose tomb is the oldest in Stillorgan Churchyard, and five cottages, inhabited by nineteen residents, of whom five were of English and fourteen of Irish extraction[142].

At the close of the eighteenth century, in 1795, the lands of Laughanstown, then held by the tenants of Brenanstown, the Mercer family, were selected as the site of the great camp, which enters so largely into the history of the Rebellion of 1798, and which is connected with the fate of the brother Sheares. It extended over 120 acres, and accommodated as many as 4,000 soldiers at the same time. The sight which it presented was until then without parallel in Ireland, and the mingling of social life with the panoply of war struck a contemporary writer as no less grotesque than novel. The camp was the scene of constant gaiety. The Lord Lieutenant, the Earl Camden, on going down to review the troops, found a breakfast the most agreeable part of the proceedings; Lord Cloncurry mentions the hospitality of the officers; and

---

[142] Christ Church Deeds; Fiants, Philip and Mary, 104, 275; Elizabeth, 1158; Fleetwood's Survey; Down Survey; Cromwellian Leases in Public Record Office; Census of 1659; Hearth Money Roll. The Tombstone in Stillorgan Churchyard bears the following inscription:— "Here under lieth the body of Edward Buller, who departed this life ye 1st of April, 16 [91], his wife, Jane Buller, alias Ferrar, caused this stone to be laid here for them and their posterity."

a gentleman who went down to see military evolutions, found that a ball, in a room specially built for dancing, had been substituted[143].

BRENANSTOWN.

THE lands of Brenanstown contain a cromlech, remarkable for its perfect condition and the size of its roof rock, which is estimated to weigh sixty tons. It stands not far from the village of Cabinteely, in the lands of Glendruid[144].

This monument indicates the existence of earlier owners, but the first mention of the lands under their present name is in the fourteenth century, when they belonged to the Priory of the Holy Trinity, and were included in the manor of Kill-of-the-Grange. At the beginning of that century they were held by Maurice Howell, a leader of the militia and large farmer, but towards the close a fortified house was built upon them, and they were leased to one of the Walshes, who was Chaplain of Tully Church. After the dissolution of the Priory the lands, which probably had remained in the occupation of the Walsh family from the fourteenth century, were held under the Chapter of the Cathedral, in 1555, by the owner of Carrickmines, William Walsh, and, in 1571, by Owen Walsh. It was then obligatory on the tenants to bring the tithe corn to a place called "the holy stood," to mow a meadow belonging to the Cathedral, and to plant twenty oak or ash trees each year. At the beginning of the seventeenth century, William Rochfort—doubtless, one of the Rochforts, of Kilbogget—through his marriage to a daughter of the house of Walsh, became tenant, as did subsequently Thomas Wolverston, a younger son of the owner of Stillorgan, on his marriage to Rochfort's second wife[145].

During the Commonwealth the lands were treated as forfeited, and were leased by the Parliament to Valentine Wood, one of the officers who had been stationed at Bullock. The population was returned as four English and fourteen Irish, inhabiting ten houses, and in addition to the castle, which had

---

[143] Ferrar's "View of Dublin," pp. 124-128; *Hibernian Magazine* for 1796, pt. ii., p. 289; "Personal Recollections of Lord Cloncurry," p. 166; MS. Diary of Alexander Hamilton, LL.D., K.C.

[144] "The Rock Monuments of the County Dublin," by Henry O'Neill, in *Journal R.S.A.I.,* vol. ii., p. 41; Borlase's "Dolmens of Ireland," vol. ii., p. 390.

[145] Christ Church Deeds; Funeral Entry in Ulster's Office.

only a thatched roof, there was a mill for cleaning wool and one for grinding corn. After the Restoration the lands, which were recovered by Dr. Lightburne, together with the tithes enjoyed by the Fagans of Bullock, under an old lease, for the Cathedral, were held by the same lessees as Killiney. The castle was for a time in the hands of the Dean of Christ Church, but, in 1683, was occupied by a family called Powell[146].

Cromlech near Brenanstown in 1775.
From a Drawing by Gabriel Beranger.

Early in the eighteenth century the castle was modernised, and was the residence for a few years before his death of an eminent Dublin physician, Dr. Francis Le Hunte, who retired from practice on succeeding, through the death of his brother, to the family estates in Wexford. The doctor is said to have been distinguished for his extensive charities, benevolence, and affability, and Mozeen, in "An Invitation to Dr. Le Hunte's" describes Brenanstown as the

---

[146] Fleetwood's Survey; Down Survey; Census of 1659; Hearth Money Roll; Monkstown Parish Register.

home of every virtue and delight[147]. After Dr. Le Hunte's death, which took place in 1750, Brenanstown was taken by Captain Luke Mercer, well known in his day as the commander of the Revenue cruisers *The Thompson* and *The Besborough*. He had been successful in seizing an enormous quantity of contraband goods, and, before taking Brenanstown, had been advanced to a higher position under the Revenue Board. He was a man of large means, and converted Brenanstown into one of the handsomest seats in the county, improving the house, and laying out gardens, which became famous for their early produce. On his death, in 1781, his property passed to his brother's son and daughter, who had married, at Brenanstown, Hugh, afterwards Viscount Carleton, and Chief Justice of the Common Pleas, and the house was occupied subsequently by, amongst others Mr. John Purdon and Major Parker[148].

KERRYMOUNT.

THESE lands, which were known as Kiltekerry, or Keatingsland, and on which there was a primitive church, were originally the property of St. Patrick's Cathedral, but were given to the Priory of the Holy Trinity at the time the church of Kill-of-the-Grange was exchanged for that of Ballymore. They were held under the Priory, with other lands, known as Priorsland, and the Common of Dromin, by the tenants of Brenanstown, until the beginning of the seventeenth century, when they were in the occupation of the owner of Stillorgan, William Wolverston. After the Restoration they were leased to the Earl of Meath, and were subsequently assigned by him to Sir Joshua Allen, the owner of Carrickmines and of Stillorgan. In the latter part of the eighteenth century Sir William Mayne, who took the title of Baron Newhaven of Carrickmines, on being created a peer, held them in right of his wife, a daughter of the second Viscount Allen[149].

---

[147] Mozeen's "Miscellaneous Essays," p. 67; *Dublin Journal*, Nos. 2007, 2116, 2476.

[148] *Pue's Occurrences*, vol. xxxiii., No. 102, vol. lii., No. 32, vol. lxiii., No. 6513; *Dublin Journal*, Nos. 1999, 2405; Will of Luke Mercer; Cooper's Note Book; Post Chaise Companion, ed. 1786 and 1806.

[149] "Leacs and Crosses of the Dublin Half Barony of Rathdown," by P. J. O'Reilly, in *Journal R.S.A.I.*, vol. xxxi., pp. 255-258; Christ Church Deeds.

Murphystown.

SOME small remains of a castle are still to be seen in the townland of Murphystown, within the grounds of Glencairn, the seat of the late Right Hon. Mr. Justice Murphy, and, in the eighteenth century, as the picture shows, ruins of much greater size were visible[150].

Murphystown Castle in 1775.
From a Drawing by Gabriel Beranger.

The modern townland of Murphystown originally formed portion of widely-extending lands called Ballyogan, which were in the possession of the Priory of the Holy Trinity shortly after the English Conquest. Part of these lands was subsequently transferred to the Cathedral of St. Patrick, and the remainder retained by the Priory was divided into two portions, represented by the townlands of Murphystown and Ballyogan. The lands comprised in

---

[150] "The Lesser Castles of the County Dublin," by E. R. M'C. Dix, in *The Irish Builder* for 1897, p. 199.

the townland of Murphystown, which had been probably leased, in 1230, to the tenant of the adjoining lands of Leopardstown, Geoffrey Tyrrel, were, in 1326, held by a relative of the tenant of Brenanstown, Peter Howell, a frequent guest at the Prior's table, and the lands comprised in the townland of Ballyogan, by Robert son of Stephen and Gilbert Begg. Towards the end of that century these lands were leased, under the names of Ballymorthan and Farnecost, to Sir John Cruise, the owner of Stillorgan, and, in the sixteenth century, were held by the Harolds, who occupied a great tract of land round the Dublin Mountains, and are commemorated in the name Harold's Cross; amongst the tenants being, in 1592, Walter Harold, whose children succeeded to the farm of Kill-of-the-Grange. In the early part of the seventeenth century the Wolverstons, of Stillorgan, were in possession of the lands, and, under the Commonwealth, John Davis and seventeen other persons were resident in Murphystown. After the Restoration Murphystown and Ballyogan were recovered, with its other adjacent property, for the Cathedral, by Dr. Lightburne, and were subsequently held by the lessees of Tipperstown[151].

LEOPARDSTOWN.

THESE lands, now forming the handsome demesne of Leopardstown Park, the seat of Mr. James Talbot Power, D.L., and the racecourse, belonging to the Leopardstown Club, were known, until the eighteenth century, when their name assumed its present meaningless form, as Leperstown. This designation the lands derived from their owner in mediæval times—the Leper Hospital of St. Stephen—an institution whose site is now occupied by Mercer's Hospital, in Dublin. Of its foundation and original constitution nothing has been ascertained, but it seems to have been under the management of a religious order, which selected the care of those afflicted with this loathsome disease as its special mission.

---

[151] "Leacs and Crosses of the Dublin Half Barony of Rathdown," by P. J. O'Reilly, in *Journal, R.S.A.I.,* .vol. xxxi., pp. 254-258; Christ Church Deeds; "Account Roll of the Priory of the Holy Trinity"; Fleetwood's Survey; Down Survey; Census of 1659; Hearth Money Roll.

The hospital is first mentioned in connection with the lands in 1230, when "the master and lepers of the house of St. Stephen, at Dublin," agreed to accept a surrender of them from Geoffry Tyrrel and his wife Sara. It probably was indebted to the family or former husband of Sara for the lands, then called Balygyregan, and it was agreed that she and her husband should occupy part of them adjacent to Kilmacud during their lives, and that afterwards this portion should be let to their children, and to a son of Sara's by her first marriage. A church, known as the Church of St. Stephen, was established at Leperstown during the next century, and the tithes of the lands, which were in possession of Ellena Mocton, a great benefactress of the hospital, and probably a descendant of the original grantor of Leperstown, were in 1378, assigned to the hospital. It has been suggested that Leperstown was the site of an auxiliary home for the lepers, but documentary evidence does not corroborate this theory. In 1400 Simon Hacket was in occupation of the lands, in 1571 Robert Walsh, and a few years later, James Wolverston, who became the owner of Stillorgan. The boundaries of the lands proved a fruitful source of litigation between the hospital and the Priory of the Holy Trinity, as owners of Tipperstown. In 1391 the Priory recovered, in a Court of Assize, held at Drogheda, from Philip, the rector of Leperstown, part of the lands of Tipperstown, and, in 1508, in a suit with John English, custos of the lepers, and a canon of St. Patrick's Cathedral, the Prior established his right to retain it[152].

At the close of the sixteenth century Leperstown, which had been leased by the Corporation of Dublin, as guardian of the property of the Leper Hospital, to the Right Hon. Jacques Wingfield, the owner of Stillorgan, was seized by the Crown and given to Sir Anthony St. Leger. But the Corporation did not recognise the right of the Crown, and with the custos of the hospital, Lancelot Money, who was a son of Mrs. Garvey, the tenant of Kill-of-the-Grange, and one of the first Fellows of Trinity College, Dublin, leased the premises to Alderman William Gough. Gough seems to have entered into an agreement with Sir Anthony St. Leger as to their purchase, and, in 1605, the Corporation issued a new lease to one of their own body, Sir John Tyrrell, sometime Mayor of Dublin, on condition that he recovered the lands from

---

[152] Christ Church Deeds; "History of St. Stephen's Hospital," by Edward Evans, in *The Irish Builder*, 1895, p. 169, 1896, p. 218; Patent Rolls, p. 157; Fiants, Elizabeth, 1783, 6411.

Gough's representatives. In this Tyrrell appears to have been unsuccessful, and, in 1623, Patrick Gough, who had in the previous year litigation about the boundaries with the Cathedral of Christ Church, leased the lands to Christopher Wolverston, brother of the owner of Stillorgan, and tenant of the farm of Kill-of-the-Grange[153].

Subsequently George Wolverston, the eldest son of the owner of Stillorgan, came to reside at Leperstown, on his marriage to a daughter of the reigning Kavanagh of Borris, who was, through her mother, a granddaughter of Viscount Mountgarret. There were then on the lands a castle and two substantial houses but no trace of them or of the chapel of Leperstown, which was served, in 1641, by the Rev. Randolph Foxwist, and in 1646 by the Rev. Thomas Walworth, is now to be found. George Wolverston died prematurely in 1634, but his family continued to occupy the lands, and soon after the establishment of the Commonwealth in 1652, Mrs. Wolverston was tried before a court-martial for giving shelter at Leperstown to a girl named Mabel Archbold, a family to which the Wolverstons were related, who was hanged as a spy, and for allowing cattle which had been stolen from an inhabitant of Newcastle to graze on her lands. She was amongst those ordered off to Connaught, but was given an extension of time for her departure, on the ground of bad weather, and possibly managed to evade the order altogether, as in 1659 her only son James, and in 1664 she herself was returned as resident at Leperstown. There was then a total population on the lands of twelve English and nine Irish. After the Restoration, the lands of Leperstown were restored, with those of Stillorgan, to James Wolverston, and during part of the eighteenth century were in the occupation of a farmer called Carty, who took part in a competition, under the auspices of the Dublin Society, for wheat grown in the County Dublin[154].

Not long before the Union Leperstown came into the possession of Colonel Charles Henry Coote, M.P. for Maryborough, who built the present house and laid out the grounds. He succeeded in 1802, on the death of his

---

[153] Gilbert's "Ancient Records of Dublin," vol. ii., pp. 308, 434; Chancery Inquisitions, Co. Dublin, Jac. I., No. 58; Christ Church Deeds.

[154] Funeral Entry in Ulster's Office; Down Survey; Fleetwood's Survey; Diocesan Records Loftus' "Court Martial Book," in Marsh's Library; Prendergast's "Cromwellian Settlement," p. xx; Census of 1659; Hearth Money Roll; *Exshaw's Magazine* for 1742, p. 572.

kinsman, the last Earl of Mountrath, to the barony of Castlecoote, and as his endowment of schools in the neighbourhood proves, was a man of large and generous mind. Leopardstown in his time was considered, as it still remains, one of the most beautiful seats in the County Dublin, and the farm and garden, which provided sheep "of the real Wicklow breed," and fruit and vegetables for the use of George IV., while he lay in his yacht in Kingstown Harbour, were noted for the luxuriance and excellence of their products[155].

Ecclesiastical History.

Ruined Church of Tully.
From a Photograph in the collection of the Royal Society of Antiquaries of Ireland.

THE ruined church of Tully lies not far from the village of Cabinteely. All that is now to be seen is the remains of the chancel, which is of Anglo-Norman

---

[155] Dublin Directory; Archer's "Survey of the County Dublin"; *Saunders's News-Letter*, Sept. 7, 1821.

construction, and contains a choir arch and round-headed window, but probably this chancel was attached to an early Celtic church, which formed the nave. Near the ruins are two crosses; one of them, which stands on the road, is a cross radiating from a circle, the other, which stands in an adjacent field is of the ordinary form, and bears in relief the figure of a female, probably a representation of St. Bridget, the patron saint of the church. In the churchyard two very early tombstones have been discovered; one is inscribed with three groups of well-defined rings, and resembles in shape a cross, and the other is inscribed with a rudely-carved cross, surrounded by a circle[156].

The antiquity of Tully as the site of a place of worship is indicated by an ancient legend, which recounts how eight holy men, or chorepiscopi, who came from the Hill of the Bishops, as Tully was anciently called, to visit St. Bridget, in the County Kildare, were miraculously provided with refreshment, and it is not improbable that Tully was in Celtic times the site of a monastery. The ruined church has been stated to be of Danish origin, and although Dr. Todd believed the statement to be devoid of foundation, the fact that the lands of Tully were given to the Priory by a Scandinavian owner, affords some ground for such a conjecture. The church was dedicated to St. Bridget, and it is possible that in its dedication and the visit of the holy men of Tully to the saint, some connection may be found. After the English Conquest Tully was assigned to the Priory of the Holy Trinity, and was attached to the mother church of Kill-of-the-Grange. In the fourteenth century the church of Tully was a centre of religious activity; it was served by a resident chaplain, and possessed a clerk. After the dissolution of the religious houses it was probably but little used. At the beginning of the seventeenth century there was not a single Protestant in the parish, and the church, owing to recent storms, was in a ruinous condition. The parish was, in 1615, in charge of the curate of Kill-of-the-Grange and Dalkey, the Rev. Owen Ellis, and later on in that of the vicar of Bray, the Rev. Simon Swayne. Under the latter it was served, in 1646, by his curate, the Rev. Thomas Walworth, who also held the curacy of Leperstown, and who, though the tithes of the parish were worth £64 a year, only received the miserable stipend of £5. Under the Commonwealth

---

[156] "Primitive Churches in the County Dublin," by W. F. Wakeman, and "Leacs and Crosses in the Dublin Half-Barony of Rathdown," by P. J. O'Reilly in *Journal R.S.A.I.*, vol. xxi., p. 700 and vol. xxxi., pp. 142, 247.

Godfrey Daniel, of Tully, was appointed by the Parliament, at a salary of £30 a year, as preacher and catechiser to the Irish in the neighbourhood, but his efforts bore little fruit. After the Restoration the church fell more and more into ruin, and the parish was united to that of Monkstown[157].

The Roman Catholic Church so long as the Walshes were at Carrickmines had the use of the castle for their services, and after the Restoration probably had concealed places of worship as, in 1704, the Rev. James Connor was returned as parish priest of Tully, and the Rev. James Murphy as parish priest of St. Stephen's of Leperstown, as well as of Kill-of-the-Grange[158].

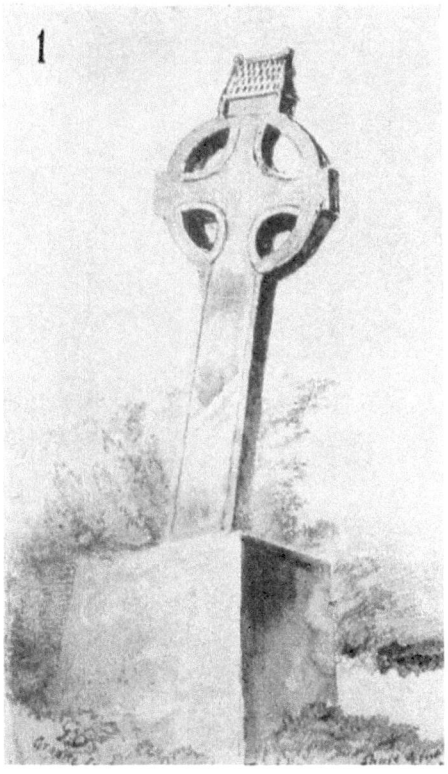

Cross on the road at Tully.
From a Drawing by G. V. Du Noyer.

---

[157] O'Hanlon's "Lives of the Irish Saints," vol. ii., p. 144; "Obits and Martyrology of Christ Church," p. 133; Christ Church Deeds; Regal Visitation of 1615; Diocesan Records; Archbishop Bulkeley's Report; Commonwealth Order Book in Public Record Office.

[158] "Return of Roman Catholic Clergy in 1704."

Cross in the Field at Tully.
From a Drawing by G. V. Du Noyer.

Stone with concentric markings at Tully.
From a Drawing by G. V. Du Noyer.

PARISH OF STILLORGAN.

Stillorgan (or Tigh Lorcain, the House of Lorcan), as shown on the Down Survey Map, comprised the modern townlands of Stillorgan, North and South, Stillorgan Grove, Stillorgan Park, Carysfort, and Woodland. It now also includes Waltersland and the Glebe.

STILLORGAN PARK.

STILLORGAN, or the House of Lorcan or Laurence, which was probably known in early times as the place of sepulchre of a chief, whose tomb was discovered in the eighteenth century in the park[159], became, under English rule, the centre of a manor held from the Crown by military service. There was to be seen, in the centuries succeeding the Conquest, a fortified house, surrounded by a bawn, with the usual manorial adjuncts of a mill and a dovecote, while not far off, on the site of the modern church, stood a primitive place of worship nestling amidst a thick wood. The manor was liable equally with those which adjoined it to the raids of the mountain tribes, and owing to its being laid waste and devastated, the rent, for which it was found convenient to commute the service of a knight and a half, was sometimes remitted by the Crown to the owner.

The first English owner appears to have been Raymond Carew, who gave portion of the original lands of Stillorgan, which extended to the sea, as mentioned under Seapoint, to St. Mary's Abbey. He was succeeded by members of the Hacket family, who were prominent people in the district, and great allies and friends of the canons at Kill-of-the-Grange. At the close of the fourteenth century the manor came into the possession of a magnate of the Pale, Sir John Cruise, who held the adjoining lands of Merrion and Booterstown, as well as those of Kilmacud and Murphystown, and who was

---

[159] Molyneux's "Discourses concerning the Danish Mounts, Forts, and Towers of Ireland," Dublin, 1725, p. 201.

distinguished both in civil and military employment. As a member of the judiciary and of the Parliament of his time, he was sent to England to report on the state of Ireland, and as one foremost in repelling the incursions of the enemies of the King, he was on one occasion severely wounded. Before his death, which took place in 1407, he had assigned the manor to John Derpatrick and his wife Maria, who was possibly a daughter of Cruise, and on Derpatrick being killed soon afterwards, in 1410, while taking part in an expedition under the Lord-Deputy against the O'Tooles, it passed to his eldest son, Robert Derpatrick.

The manor house was, in 1422, occupied by the principal tenant, John Loghenan, but portion of the lands was retained by the owner, and was doubtless cultivated for him by his tenants, who comprised besides Loghenan, another Englishman, Richard Locumbe, and two Irishmen. Robert Derpatrick, who had married a daughter of the Chief Baron of the Exchequer, James Uriell, had died before that time, leaving an only daughter, and as the manor was entailed in the male line, his brother Stephen succeeded to it. Stephen was then a minor, and for some years the manor was vested in Bartholomew de Bathe, of Drumcondra (who had married Robert Derpatrick's widow) and other trustees, and was the subject of much litigation. Not long after he came of age. Stephen Derpatrick committed some crime, which led to his being proclaimed an outlaw, and the manor then reverted to the Cruise family. Subsequently, through the marriage of Sir Christopher Cruise's only daughter to Sir Thomas Plunkett, Chief Justice of the King's Bench in the reign of Edward IV., the manor came into the possession of the Plunketts of Rathmore, from whom sprang the noble houses of Dunsany, Killeen, and Louth, and remained their property for more than one hundred and fifty years[160]

The latter part of the sixteenth century saw the settlement at Stillorgan of a branch of the ancient Suffolk family of Wolverston, or Wolferston, and the

---

[160] "The Norman Settlement in Leinster," by James Mills, in *Journal R.S.A.I.*, vol. xxiv., p. 173; "Chartularies of St. Mary's Abbey," vol. i., p. 111; Sweetman's "Calendar of Documents relating to Ireland," 1293-1301, p. 108; Patent and Close Rolls; D'Alton's "History of the County Dublin," pp. 26-29; and "King James' Irish Army List," pp. 567-568; Burke's "Peerage and Baronetage" under de Bathe; Lodge's "Peerage of Ireland," edited by Mervyn Archdall, vol. vi., p. 181; "Dublin University Magazine," vol. xliv., p. 320.

granting by the Plunketts of a lease of the manor and lands to the Right Hon. Jacques Wingfield. Both of these events were probably due to the residence in the neighbouring castle of Monkstown of the Master of the Ordnance, Sir John Travers. The Wolverstons, who first appear as resident at Stillorgan, had served under Travers, and Wingfield had discharged Travers' duties for some years before his death, and afterwards succeeded to his office. At the time of Wingfield's death, in 1587, the Wolverstons were probably his tenants for the lands of Stillorgan. The state of his department, of which he had only retained control through the soundness of his patent and his interest with his relative, Lord Burghley, had long been the source of complaint, and owing to confusion in his accounts, Stillorgan with the rest of his property was seized by the Crown[161]. It was, however, soon surrendered to the Plunketts, and in the following year was leased by them to James Wolverston, who was then residing at Leopardstown.

James Wolverston was the son of George Wolverston, who married one of the Rochforts, of Kilbogget, and who had displayed much valour as captain of the O'Byrne's country. Like most of his family, James Wolverston saw military service, but after he had acquired Stillorgan, he devoted himself with success to the improvement of his worldly circumstances. At the time of his death, in 1609, he had become a man of note in the county. He was in occupation of lands in the County Wicklow, as well as in the County Dublin, and was owner of several studs of horses, herds of cattle, flocks of sheep, and droves of pigs, besides great store of corn, much household stuff, and plate. These he divided between his widow, a daughter of Richard Archbold, the owner of the adjoining lands of Kilmacud, and his four sons, William, who became owner of Stillorgan; Robert, who succeeded to lands near Baltinglass; Christopher, who settled on the farm of Kill-of-the-Grange, and John, who succeeded to lands near Newcastle[162].

.

---

[161] Burke's "Landed Gentry" under Wolferston; Bagwell's "Ireland under the Tudors," vols. ii. and iii.; "Calendar of State Papers, Ireland;" "Calendar of Carew State Papers;" Lodge's "Peerage of Ireland," edited by Mervyn Archdall, vol. v., p. 267.

[162] Chancery Inquisitions, Co. Dublin, Jac. I., No. 36; Fiants; "Calendar of State Papers, Ireland," 1586-1588, p. 41; Wills of the Wolverstons; Funeral Entries in Ulster's Office; "The Description of Ireland in 1598," edited by Rev. Edmund Hogan, p. 37.

Dublin Bay from Stillorgan Road in 1795.
From a Plate drawn by F. Jukes.

The manor house of Stillorgan in the sixteenth century was the largest in the neighbourhood, excepting the castle of Monkstown, and was surrounded by extensive offices and gardens, while a little way off an orchard and a grove of ash trees hid from view the mill, which was still in use, on one of the little streams. Its new owner, William Wolverston, lost no opportunity of adding to the lands which he had inherited from his father, and purchased from the Plunketts the fee of Stillorgan. He was, in his time, one of the most prominent residents, and the most striking personality, in the southern portion of the County Dublin. Like his neighbours, the Cheevers, the Goodmans, and the Walshes, he was a Roman Catholic. His family had been Protestant, but through intermarriage with early English settlers, had become Roman Catholic, and Wolverston was a most devout son of the latter church, maintaining a priest in his house at Stillorgan, and showing much hospitality to travelling friars, who returned, we are told, to their monasteries enriched, not only with his benefactions, but also with those of the poorer people. The Rebellion of 1641 found him residing at Stillorgan. Related as he was, through his mother, and his grandmother, and through his wife, one of the Barnewalls of Shankill, to the Walshes, the Rochforts, and other leaders in the rising, his sympathy must have been largely with the rebel side, but he kept himself clear from any overt act of rebellion. He did not, however, escape without suspicion. The curate of Kill-of-the-Grange deposed that when the rebels carried off his wife, they brought her across bogs which then lay between that place and Stillorgan, to Wolverston's house, and that, though Wolverston desired them not to hang her on his own lands, he took no steps to prevent their doing so at Powerscourt. Possibly he was not in a position to oppose their designs, but in consequence of Mr. Smithson's allegations, he was arrested and confined in Dublin Castle until Lord Clanricarde, under whom one of Wolverston's sons was then serving, wrote to the Marquis of Ormonde, begging for his release, on the ground of his being a man of good repute, and well disposed to the King's cause[163].

William Wolverston's death took place two years later, in 1644, and his property passed to his grandson, James, the son of George Wolverston, of Leopardstown. As his grandson was then a minor, the lands were vested in the

---

[163] Fleetwood's Survey; Down Survey; Archbishop Bulkeley's Report; Depositions of 1641; "Memoirs and Letters of Ulick, Marquis of Clanricarde," London, 1757, p. 267.

Marquis of Ormonde who, occupied as he was with more weighty matters, can hardly have given much attention to them, and probably they were utterly derelict when the Commonwealth was established. They were subsequently assigned by the Parliament to Major Henry Jones, who was arrested in 1663 for complicity in Blood's plot to take Dublin Castle. Jones was residing at Stillorgan at the time of his arrest, but shortly before a decree of innocence had been obtained by James Wolverston from the Commissioners of Settlement, and under it Jones' widow and children were evicted from the house and lands[164].

James Wolverston, on taking up his residence at Stillorgan, found, as Cheevers had done at Monkstown, that his property had not suffered during the Cromwellian occupation. The village at the time of the Restoration contained eighteen houses, and there was a population of some thirteen English and twenty-five Irish. He did not, however, long enjoy his recovered possessions, and died three years later, in 1666, when only 36 years of age. His widow, a sister of the tenth Lord Dunsany, married soon after his death Bryan O'Neill, of Upper Claneboys, who succeeded to the baronetcy conferred upon his father after the battle of Edgehill, and became, in the reign of James II., one of the judges of the King's Bench. For a time the O'Neills occupied Stillorgan, but prior to the accession of James II. it came into the possession of Sir Joshua Allen[165].

The first of the Allen family (which became identified with Stillorgan and converted the lands into one of the finest demesnes in the County Dublin) to settle in Ireland was a certain John Allen, who modestly describes himself as a bricklayer, but who was one of the most eminent master builders or architects of his day. He is said to have come to Dublin from Holland, where he probably acquired his knowledge of building, but soon was successful in obtaining much employment in Dublin—success to which his handsome person, as Lodge quaintly tells us, largely contributed. Amongst those by whom he was employed was the Earl of Strafford, who confided to him the erection of the mansion which he began to build near Naas. Sir Joshua Allen

---

[164] Historical Manuscripts Commission, Rept. 8, App., pp. 502, 512, 541; Carte Papers; Decree of Innocents, IV., 17.

[165] Census of 1659; Hearth Money Roll; Subsidy Rolls; Lodge's "Peerage of Ireland," edited by Mervyn Archdall, vol. vi., p. 211.

was his eldest son. At the time of his father's death, in 1641, he was only a child, but he was brought up by his mother, in accordance with his father's injunctions, with tender care, and in the Protestant religion, and on attaining to manhood he displayed great business capacity. He soon acquired an ample fortune, and took a foremost place amongst Dublin citizens. As a prominent member of the Corporation he was elected successively Sheriff and Mayor, and during his tenure of the latter office received from the Lord Lieutenant, the Earl of Essex, to whom he presented the freedom of the city in a gold box, the honour of knighthood. Soon after James II. had ascended the throne, Allen foresaw the coming troubles, and though then extensively engaged in business, began to entertain an idea of removing to England. The Lord Lieutenant, the Earl of Clarendon, who says that Allen was as wise a man of his profession as could be met with, and of as clear a reputation as anyone in this kingdom, tried to dissuade him from taking this step, and begged him to lay aside gloomy apprehensions, but Allen was not to be deceived by fair words, and before James II. came to Ireland he took refuge in Chester, to which place his wife's family belonged. There he came into touch with William III., and acted as his agent in making arrangements for the embarkation of that monarch's troops for Ireland. He returned to Ireland after the Battle of the Boyne, and was appointed the first Sheriff of Dublin under William III, but as his death took place in the following year he did not live to reap the fruits of that victory[166].

It was Sir Joshua Allen's intention to form the lands of Stillorgan and of Carrickmines, which he purchased at the same time, and which were connected with those of Stillorgan by the lands which he leased from Christ Church Cathedral, into a manorial estate and great family seat, and with this object he reserved in the patent which he obtained from the Crown, the right to enclose a demesne and deer park. He lived in times, however, which were not favourable to the execution of such a design, and it was left to his son, Colonel John Allen, to carry out his project, at any rate in part. This Colonel Allen did, by the erection at Stillorgan of a stately mansion. Its ruins, which

---

[166] Lodge's "Peerage of Ireland," edited by Mervyn Archdall, vol. v., p. 181; Will of John Allen; Gilbert's "Calendar of Ancient Records of Dublin"; Carte Papers; "Letters of Henry Hyde, Earl of Clarendon, and Lawrence Hyde, Earl of Rochester," edited by S. W. Singer, vol. i., p. 572, vol. ii., p. 150; Calendar of State Papers, William and Mary.

stood on the site of the residence known as Park House, and which bore the date of its construction, 1695, have only disappeared within the last quarter of a century. The mansion, which faced the north, consisted of a central building, three stories in height, from which wings, two stories in height, extended on either side. The central building projected from the wings, and was connected by curtain walls, which encircled a large courtyard, with a miniature theatre and out-offices. In appearance the mansion has been compared to one made of cards, and as the picture indicates, the comparison was not altogether without justification. It was surrounded by extensive gardens, covering thirteen acres, which were laid out in Dutch style, probably by an Englishman called Bullein, who was the principal rural artist in Ireland at that time. The gardens abounded in straight avenues and alleys, with curious edgings of box, carefully clipped yew trees, knots of flowers, topiary work, and grassy slopes, and possibly there may have been, as there was in Bullein's nursery, the representation of a boar hunt or hare chase cut out in box.

Stillorgan House circa 1830.

Three artificial fish ponds, laid out, like everything else, on strictly rectangular lines, lay to the south of the house on the other side of an eminence in the undulating surface of the park. The approach to them from the house was through a remarkable passage and tunnel, the only remaining relic of the occupation of the Allens, which were cut through the mound and in the excavations for which it is probable that the tomb, already referred to, was found. The walls of the passage and tunnel were built of brick, and were decorated with niches, tablets, and sculptural figures, apparently designed on some classic model. The remaining lands of Stillorgan were converted into a great park, which stretched away on the south to Newtown Park Avenue, on the north to Merrion Avenue, and on the east to Blackrock. The portion now occupied by the grounds of Obelisk Park, and of Carysfort House and by Newtown Park village, were enclosed for deer, and a handsome avenue bordered with elm trees was made towards Merrion Avenue[167].

Entrance to Grotto in Stillorgan Park.

---

[167] Grant under Commission of Grace; Lease in Registry of Deeds Office; "Autobiography and Correspondence of Mary Granville, Mrs. Delany," vol. i., p. 373; Walker's "Essay on Gardening in Ireland," in *Transactions, Royal Irish Academy* Antiquities, vol. iv., p. 13; Loudon's "Encyclopædia of Gardening," p. 83.

Grotto in Stillorgan Park.

Colonel John Allen had served in King William's army, and displayed through life a rigid adherence to the principles which actuated his conduct in early days. As owner of the Stillorgan and Carrickmines estate, he was recognised as one of the leading men in the metropolitan county, and was returned to the first Irish Parliament under William III. as one of its representatives. From that time he became immersed in politics. For twenty-five years he occupied a seat in the House of Commons; during three Parliaments as representative of the County Dublin, during one as representative of the County Carlow, and during another as representative for the County Wicklow. He largely increased the estate, which included lands in the County Kildare, left him by his father, and purchased, in addition to the property at Bullock and Dalkey, the town and lands of Arklow, in the County Wicklow, now owned, as well as the former, by his descendant the Earl of Carysfort. Besides the influence derived from his territorial possessions, Colonel Allen had formed an alliance with one of the most powerful families of his day by his marriage to the sister of Robert, the nineteenth Earl of

Kildare, and his distinguished brother-in-law was a constant guest at Stillorgan. We find him staying there in 1714, on the accession of George I., when he was appointed one of the Lords Justices, and again in 1719, when one of his children was baptized in Monkstown Church. Colonel Allen strenuously exerted himself to secure the peaceful succession of the House of Hanover. He was one of the principal witnesses against the Rev. Francis Higgins, who has been called the "Irish Sacheverel," and steadfastly set his face against the Jacobite tendencies of Queen Anne's Ministers. At the General Election in 1713 he used his wealth to obtain the return to Parliament of members sharing his views. His eldest son was then elected for the County Kildare, and his second son for the borough of Carysfort, in the County Wicklow, while by the return, at the General Election on the accession of George I., of his youngest son for the borough of Athy, the unusual spectacle was witnessed of a father and three sons all sitting in Parliament at the same time, and, still more remarkable, all returned unopposed. A Privy Councillorship was Allen's immediate reward, and three years later a peerage was conferred upon him as Baron Allen of Stillorgan and Viscount Allen of Kildare[168].

Joshua, the second Viscount Allen, succeeded to Stillorgan on his father's death, which occurred in London in 1726, and he resided there constantly. He has gained an unenviable notoriety as the subject of some of Swift's severest satires. The Dean does not allow him the possession of a single good quality; but two letters of his, written from abroad in early life to his friend Joshua Dawson, the Secretary to the Lords Justices, exhibit inherent discretion and a spirit of patriotism in the passionate wish he expresses to be amongst his Dublin friends again "in a little hole about ye Round Church." He was certainly easily led; and it is said that his marriage, which took place in 1707, when he was twenty-two years of age, was the result of a trick played upon him by his friend Lionel Sackville, afterwards Duke of Dorset. It is related that at first he refused to acknowledge the lady, a Miss Du Pass, a relative of the Welbore Ellis family, as his wife, but on her inserting a notice in the newspapers stating that she had succeeded to a large fortune he became as

---

[168] Return of Members of Ireland; Mant's "History of the Church of Ireland," vol. p. 227; "Account of the Trial of the Rev. Francis Higgins"; "Dictionary of National Biography," vol. xxvi., p. 367.

desirous to prove the marriage as he had previously been to disown it, and before he found out that the report was without foundation the lady had gained complete ascendancy over him. Lady Allen, although a warm friend and affectionate wife, was a masterful woman and as regards her influence with her husband there can be no doubt[169].

It was probably by the second Lord Allen, during a great famine in 1727, that the Obelisk which now stands in the grounds of Obelisk Park, and was long the pride of the neighbourhood, and the most conspicuous object in the surrounding country, was erected. It is traditionally reported to have been designed by Sir Edward Lovet Pearce, the architect of the Irish House of Commons, and this report is more or less confirmed by the fact that Pearce came to reside about that time in a house within the Allen's park, then and until lately known as the Grove, and now as Tigh Lorcain Hall. The obelisk resembles, in its massive style and in its excellent state of preservation, the great work of Pearce's life. It is more than 100 feet high of cut granite, and rises from a rustic base formed of huge uncut rocks, containing a large vaulted chamber, and having on each side a double staircase leading to a platform, from which four doorways of Egyptian design furnish the entrance to a small room in the obelisk[170].

The second Lord Allen and his wife, who is said to have been much admired by the Viceroy, their old friend Lionel. Duke of Dorset, were prominent figures in the Dublin society of their day, and Stillorgan was in their time the scene of many fashionable and festive gatherings. Thither rode the good Archbishop King (who did not hesitate to apply for some of the famous Stillorgan venison, on which to feast his friends at the Visitation of Marsh's Library), to solicit Lord Allen's interest for a parliamentary candidate. There was welcomed the witty Dean, whose friendship Lord Allen at first caressed and courted, but whose enmity he was rash enough subsequently to incur by "rattling him bitterly under various injurious appellations." Thither went along the road from Dublin, which then commanded "a very fine and

---

[169] Scott's "Works of Swift," vol. vii., p. 276; vol. xii, p. 424; British Departmental Correspondence in Public Record Office; "Letters of Mary Lepel, Lady Hervey," pp. 236, 289.

[170] Lecky's "History of England in the Eighteenth Century," vol. ii., p. 217; Leases in Registry of Deeds Office; "Dictionary of National Biography," vol. xliv. p. 149.

charming prospect of the sea all the way," Mrs. Clayton in her great coach drawn "by six flouncing Flanders mares which outlooked everyone else's." And there came to stay for some weeks that gallant soldier and brilliant diplomatist, the second Earl of Stair, escorted from Donaghadee, where he had landed, by many persons of great quality and distinction[171].

Obelisk at Stillorgan in 1795.
From a Plate drawn by F. Jukes.

Lady Allen maintained her ascendancy over her husband until his death, which occurred at Stillorgan in 1742, and by a will of a few lines he bequeathed her all his property, real as well as personal. He left a son and two daughters. The son, John, third Viscount Allen, only survived his father three years, and as he had not married, the titles passed to his cousin, the son of the first Viscount's youngest son, who had succeeded to the Kildare estate. Lady Allen removed to London after her husband's death, and there her eldest daughter married Sir John Proby, who became the first Baron of Carysfort,

---

[171] Craik's "Life of Swift," p. 430; *Dublin Evening Post*, July 18-22, 1733; Archbishop King's Correspondence in Trinity College Library; "Autobiography and Correspondence of Mary Granville, Mrs. Delany," vol. i., pp. 300, 373; *Pue's Occurrences*, vol. xxxvi., Nos. 67, 74; "Dictionary of National Biography," vol. xiii, p. 420.

and her youngest, "a little lively sort of fairy," Sir William Mayne, who was also created a peer as Baron Newhaven, a title which became extinct on his death[172].

Stillorgan House and grounds were, in 1754, let to the Right Hon. Philip Tisdal, who was then Solicitor-General and Judge of the Prerogative Court, and became Attorney-General and Secretary of State; and for twenty-three years, until his death, it continued to be the country residence of that remarkable man. "He was a man of first-rate talents, and one of the greatest lawyers of his time," writes his rival Prime-Serjeant and Provost Hutchinson, "and in the courts of Justice, the Senate, the Privy Council, and the Cabinet, maintained to the time of his death the reputation of a man of great knowledge and ability." Tisdal understood so well the farce and fallacy of life, we are told, that he went through the world with a constant sunshine of soul and an inexorable gravity of feature, viewing life as if it had been a scenic representation, and he was in some respects one of the most singular, as he was undoubtedly one of the most able Irish statesmen of the eighteenth century. He lived in a style of the greatest splendour and magnificence, and during his occupation Stillorgan House was the centre of that unbounded hospitality in which he delighted. There he entertained the Lords Lieutenants of the day—in 1755 the Marquis of Hartington, in 1765 the Earl of Hertford, and frequently, during his Viceroyalty, the Marquis of Townshend, who appreciated Tisdal's well-known cook and the company of an eight bottle man, such as Tisdal is said to have been. There, also, met a small circle of political friends—"the Cabal at Stillorgan"—whom Tisdal was said to attract round him by his profusion, and whose meetings were regarded with suspicion by his rivals. And there, as his guest, Angelica Kauffmann exercised her great talents[173].

After Tisdal's death, which occurred at Spa, where he went every year, in 1777, the second Baron Carysfort, who was an active politician and

---

[172] Will of Joshua, 2nd Viscount Allen; "Autobiography and Correspondence of Mary Granville, Mrs. Delany," vol. iv., p. 438; Cokayne's "Complete Peerage."

[173] Stubbs' "History of the University of Dublin," p. 236; Hardy's "Memoirs of Charlemont," vol. i. p. 152; "Dictionary National Biography," vol. lvi. ,,p 415; *Pue's Occurrences,* vol. liv No. 74, vol. lxii., No. 6430; *Freeman's Journal,* No. 1117; Gerard's "Life of Angelica Kauffman," p 136.

diplomatist, as well as an author, and who was advanced to the dignity of an Earl, resided for a time in Stillorgan House, which he had inherited through his mother[174]. But the place was soon again let—to the Lord Chancellor of the day, the Right Hon. James Hewitt, Baron Lifford, who had previously rented Santry Court as his country residence. Lord Lifford's appointment to the Chancellorship had been much resented on the ground of his being an Englishman, but by the ability with which he discharged the business of his court, and by his upright and amiable disposition, he gained the respect both of the Bar and of the public. With the help of a young and handsome wife he dispensed much hospitality at Stillorgan, and, though his entertainments lacked the brilliancy of Tisdal's they were as frequently graced by the presence of the Viceroy, then often a near neighbour of the Chancellor's at Seapoint[175].

The outlying portions of Stillorgan Park had been advertised for building after Tisdal's death, and before the end of the eighteenth century, Carysfort Avenue had been made, and Stillorgan Castle and Carysfort House built. The grounds of Stillorgan House, to which a new approach through handsome iron gates had been constructed, retained much of their beauty, until the time of Lord Lifford's death in 1789, but under his successor, Nicholas Le Fevre, the place became much deteriorated. Le Fevre was a lottery merchant in Dublin, and carried on his business in a house at the corner of Grafton-street and Suffolkstreet[176]. In his time the other residents at Stillorgan included the Hon. Chichester Skeffington, M.P. for Antrim, and afterwards fourth Earl of Massareene; Alderman Nathaniel Warren, M.P. for Dublin, and afterwards for Callan, who resided in the house next the church now known as Woodview; and Alderman Caleb Jenkins, a well-known bookseller, who lived at the Grove, which had been occupied for many years after Sir Edward

---

[174] Taylor and Skinner's Maps; Historical Manuscripts Commission, Report 12, App., pt. x., vol. p. 374; "Dictionary of National Biography," vol. xliv., p. 414.

[175] "Post Chaise Companion," ed. 1786; Adams' "History of Santry," p. 25; Colvile's "Worthies of Warwickshire," p. 397; Dictionary of National Biography, vol. xxvi., p. 308; Hist0rical Manuscript Commission, Rept. 12, App., pt. ix., p. 276, Rept. 14, App, pt. i. vol. iii., p. 322.

[176] *Dublin Journal,* No. 6867; Archer's "Survey of the County Dublin"; Dutton's "Observations on Archer's Survey"; Picture of Grafton-street in 1770; Leases in Registry of Deeds Office.

Pearce's death by the first Sir George Ribton and his successor in the baronetcy[177].

Le Fevre came to financial grief, and his mortgagees in 1803 assigned Stillorgan House to Mr. John Verschoyle, brother of Dr. James Verschoyle, Bishop of Killala, and father of Dr. Hamilton Verschoyle, Bishop of Kilmore[178]. Carysfort House, now the Convent of Mercy, was, about the same time, taken by the Right Hon. William Saurin, one of the most distinguished lawyers the Irish Bar has ever known, and was occupied by him and his family for the greater part of the last century[179]. Stillorgan Castle, then known as Mount Eagle, and now as the House of St. John of God, was occupied at the time Mr. Verschoyle came to Stillorgan House by Mr. William Monck Mason, the author of the "History of St. Patrick's Cathedral," and subsequently by the witty Henry Deane Grady, in whose time it was known, on account of the great marriages made by his daughters, as "the House of Lords."[180] The Priory, which obtained its name from some ruins in the grounds marked on the Ordnance map as a monastery, was also built about this time, and was for many years the residence of the Right Hon. Anthony Blake, one of the founders of the National System of Education, and subsequently of Mr. William Pierce Mahony, a celebrated solicitor[181]. After Mr. Verschoyle's death, in 1840, Stillorgan House was sold to Mr. Arthur Lee Guinness, brother of Sir Benjamin Lee Guinness, who restored the place to some of its former magnificence, and revived its reputation for lavish hospitality. The house remained in his possession for about twenty years, and on the termination of his tenancy was allowed to fall gradually into ruin, until finally its walls were levelled with the ground.

---

[177] Watson's Almanac; Post Chaise Companion, ed. 1786; *Hibernian Magazine,* 1792, pt. i., p. 296; Leases in Registry of Deeds Office.

[178] See Burke's "Landed Gentry."

[179] "Dictionary of National Biography," vol. l., p. 333.

[180] Leases in Registry of Deeds Office; "Dictionary of National Biography," vol. xxxvi., p. 441; O'Flanagan's "Irish Bar," p. 204, and "Munster Circuit," p. 241.

[181] *Dublin Evening Post,* Jan. 13, 1849; Maddyn's "Chiefs of Parties," vol. ii., pp. 140, 147; "Ireland and its Rulers," vol. i., p. 196.

Ecclesiastical History.

THE origin of the name Stillorgan, or the House of Lorcan or Laurence, has been attributed to the erection of its ancient church, by St. Laurence O'Toole, who was Archbishop of Dublin at the time of the English invasion[182]. The first mention of this church, which stood on the site of the present one and was dedicated to St. Bridget, is in 1216, when Raymond Carew granted it, together with the church fields, to the Priory of the Holy Trinity. It was then attached to the mother church of Kill-of-the-Grange, and continued under it for the next 300 years. It was served by a resident chaplain, who held the church lands, and like the other churches under the Priory was, in the fourteenth century, a subject of contention with the Archdeacon of Dublin as to his right of visitation. After the dissolution of the religious houses it was allowed to fall into ruin, and was leased, together with the manse and lands, by the Chapter of Christ Church Cathedral, to various persons. Amongst these were the tenants of Stillorgan, the Right Hon. Jacques Wingfield, and the Wolverstons, who were all buried with heraldic honours in the ruined church. Also for a time the premises were leased to Alison and Katherine Ussher, two maiden aunts of Archbishop James Ussher, who are said to have taught him to read. These ladies held a lease of the tithes, which they bequeathed to their nephew by marriage, the Rev. James Donelan. During the Commonwealth Mr. Thomas Hickes was appointed, at a salary of £120 a year, "by the Church of Christ, sitting at Chichester House," to preach the Gospel at Stillorgan and other places in the barony of Rathdown. After the Restoration the parish, with that of Kilmacud, was united to Monkstown[183].

The modern church of Stillorgan is one of those which the diocese owes to the energy of Archbishop King, and was probably erected by him in concert with Colonel Allen, for whom he had a great esteem. As in other cases, the

---

[182] A headstone with "rude circles," similar to the stones at Tully, was in 1781 discovered in Stillorgan Churchyard by Mr. Austin Cooper.

[183] Joyce's "Irish Names of Places," ed. 1895, vol. i., p. 65; Archdall's "Monasticon Hibernicum," edited by Archbishop Moran, vol. ii., p. 1; Christ Church Deeds; Funeral Entries, Ulster's Office; Ball Wright's "Ussher Memoirs," p. 41; Prendergast's "Cromwellian Settlement," p. 24; Commonwealth Papers in Public Record Office.

Archbishop found it impossible to secure a provision for a resident clergyman, and it was more than fifty years before one was appointed. The church, which had meantime fallen into disrepair, was then restored by the liberality of Lord Chancellor Jocelyn, who was living at Mount Merrion and other residents, and the parishes of Stillorgan and Kilmacud were severed from Monkstown, and assigned to the charge of a separate curate. The right of presentation was vested in the Dean of Christ Church, and in 1764 was exercised in favour of the Rev. Beather King, who also held the curacy of St. John's Church, Dublin. King showed much vigour in his charge of the cure; he erected a glebe house on land, which belonged to Christ Church Cathedral, in Newtown Park Avenue, and his church was several times chosen by bishops for the purpose of ordination services. He resigned in 1785, and was succeeded by the Rev. Edward Beatty, then assistant curate of Monkstown, in whose time the tower and northern aisle were added to the church. His successors in the incumbency have been—in 1815, the Rev. Rawdon Griffith Greene; in 1839, the Rev. James Kelly; in 1845, the Rev. John Grant; in 1856, the Rev. Thomas Sill Grey; in 1872, the Rev. St. George French; and in 1879, the Rev. James Houghton Kennedy[184].

---

[184] Mant's "History of the Church of Ireland," vol. ii., p. 204; *Dublin Gazette,* No. 398; Hughes' "History of St. John's Church" Diocesan Records; Minutes of Board of First Fruits in Public Record Office.

PARISH OF KILMACUD.

The Parish is now divided into the Townlands of Kilmacud East and Kilmacud West.

Kilmacud.

THE lands of Kilmacud, or the Church of Macud, were granted after the English Conquest, together with the lands which lay between Stillorgan and Dublin, to Walter de Rideleford, Lord of Bray, and became part of the manor of Thorncastle, now represented by Booterstown. As portion of that manor they were, in the fourteenth century, in the possession of Sir John Cruise, and subsequently passed to the Fitzwilliams of Merrion, from whom the Earl of Pembroke is descended in the female line. During the fifteenth century the lands, on which there were two stone houses, were held under the Fitzwilliams, by the tenants of Shanganagh, and their trustees, Thomas Sale, of Salestown, and William Walter, a clergyman; and in the sixteenth and seventeenth century by the Archbolds[185].

The Archbolds of Kilmacud, who held the lands for more than 200 years, were descended from some of the first English settlers in the County Dublin, and belonged to a widespreading clan. The earlier members of the family were evidently, from the funeral pomp with which they were laid to rest in the quiet churchyard of Dundrum, people of good position amongst the Roman Catholic families of the Pale, and the later members were recognised amongst the landed gentry in the County Dublin, and in the County Kildare, where a branch of the family settled. Amongst the residents at Kilmacud we find, in 1584, Richard Archbold, whose daughter married James Wolverston, of Stillorgan, and whose son Piers was granted a pardon by the Crown; in 1615,

---

[185] "The Norman Settlement in Leinster," by James Mills, in *Journal, R.S.A.I.*, vol. xxiv. p. 167; Cokayne's "Complete Peerage," vol. i., p. xiii.

Patrick and Edmund Archbold; and in 1641, Maurice, son of Patrick Archbold. After the Restoration Kilmacud, which had been assigned by the Parliament to one of the regicides, John Hewson, who was governor of Dublin, was claimed under the Act of Settlement in equal shares by Gerrard Archbold, of Eadestown, in the County Kildare, "an innocent Roman Catholic," and Richard Archbold, of Mapas, in Cheshire, "an innocent Protestant." The former claimed as representative of Edmund Archbold, the joint owner in 1615, whose son William Archbold, of Cloghran, had sold his interest to Gerrard Archbold's father, and the latter as representative of Maurice Archbold, who was his grandfather. Richard Archbold was restored to his moiety of the lands; but the other moiety was confiscated and was granted by Charles II. to his brother, the Duke of York, afterwards James II.[186].

There were then four houses on the lands, and a population of thirteen persons, eleven of whom were of English extraction, and two of Irish. The Archbolds, who rented the moiety granted to the Duke of York, in addition to the moiety which they owned, continued to reside at Kilmacud. In 1681 Christopher Archbold was resident there, and in 1703, when James the Second's moiety was sold, at Chichester House, to the Hollow Sword Blade Company, which purchased a considerable quantity of his property, Mortagh Griffin, as guardian to his stepson, James Archbold, was returned as the tenant. After the death of the last of the Archbolds, who resided at Kilmacud, John Archbold, who died in 1756, their interest passed through mortgages which they had executed upon the property, into the possession of Lieutenant-Colonel John Arabin, the father-in-law of General Aylercorn, of Seapoint[187].

The house known as Redesdale, for many years the residence of Archbishop Whately, was originally the country seat of Sir Michael Smith, who held successively the judicial positions of a Baron of the Exchequer and Master of the Rolls, and whose son and grandson afterwards adorned the Irish

---

[186] Fiants, Elizabeth, No. 4405; Chancery Inquisition Co. Dublin, Jac. I., No 40; Funeral Entry in Ulster's Office; Ball and Hamilton's "Parish of Taney"; Fleetwood's Survey; Carte Papers; Decrees of Innocents, i., 56, 59; Certificate for Adventurers and Soldiers, i., 58.

[187] Census of 1659; Hearth Money Roll; Monkstown Parish Register; D'Alton's "King James' Irish Army List," p. 274; Book of Postings and Sales; *Pue's Occurrences*, vol. liii., No. 68; Assignment of Mortgage in Registry of Deeds Office.

Bench. Having been in 1799 disposed of by him, it was occupied during his short tenure of the Great Seal of Ireland, by Lord Redesdale, from whom it doubtless obtained its name, and who is said to have become so attached to the place that he shed tears on leaving it[188].

ECCLESIASTICAL HISTORY.

THE church, which stood upon the lands of Kilmacud, and which was founded by some holy man, of whom all trace is lost, was given, together with its tithes, by Walter de Rideleford to the Convent of Grany, near Castledermot, in the County Kildare, and was held by that establishment until the dissolution of the religio The Church of Clonkeenus houses. It was in the middle ages an important charge, and in 1281 its chaplain, Elias de Kilmacud, who acted as agent on behalf of the convent, was a well-known person. After the suppression of the monasteries the tithes were granted to Sir Anthony St. Leger, the Lord-Deputy of Ireland, in recompense for his services in the reformation of the country and establishment of the Government, and were sold by him to the De Bathes, of Drumcondra, who subsequently assigned them to Christ Church Cathedral. The spiritual charge of the parish under the Established Church, which was sometimes assumed by the clergy of Donnybrook or Dundrum, was given after the dissolution of the religious houses to the curate of Kill-of-the-Grange, and after the Restoration became vested in the curate of Monkstown. On the appointment of a perpetual curate of Stillorgan, the charge was assigned to him, and subsequently was given to the clergy of Dundrum[189].

---

[188] Leases in Registry of Deeds Office; "Dictionary of National Biography," vol. liii., p. 155, vol. xxxviii., p. 80; "Falkland's Review of the Irish House of Commons," p. 21; Ryan's "Worthies of Ireland," vol. ii., p. 557; Milner's "Inquiry Concerning Ireland," p. 39; "Public Characters of 1807," p. 171; "Detail of Facts relating to Ireland, particularly for the last forty years," Dublin, 1822.

[189] Archdall's "Monasticon Hibernicum," edited by Archbishop Moran, vol. ii., p. 259; Sweetman's "Calendar of Documents relating to Ireland," 1252-1284, p. 372, 1293-1301, p. 1302-1307, p. 239; Christ Church Deeds; Fiants.

www.ingramcontent.com/pod-product-compliance
Lightning Source LLC
Chambersburg PA
CBHW020425010526
44118CB00010B/418